Glorious stories

to embrace your Frenchness

By Emmanuel Adnot

"Le sourire de l'éternité se trouve dans la transmission"
- Didier Lockwood, French jazz violinist (1956 – 2018)

Foreword

It all started in London when the ambition to launch a French fast-casual food business led to the creation of the company brand *"30 Glorieuses"* (aka *"30"*): an inspirational name intended not only to celebrate food but also the French culture. The project could not be funded but the articles written for its blog remain. Here they are, a collection of stories from a French expat eager to share tales about his country – enjoy!

I dedicate this book to my daughters Florencia and Françoise, who will hopefully never stop loving their French roots and embracing their Frenchness.

Emmanuel Adnot

TABLE OF CONTENTS

THE GLORIOUS THIRTY
#History

1. Remember "Les Trente Glorieuses" aka "The Glorious Thirty"

Referring to the thirty exciting and prosperous years of France from the early fifties to the late seventies, these decades of prosperity combined fantastic economic growth with a deep transformation of society (e.g., the emancipation of women, the birth of mass consumption, and the emergence of new ground-breaking art). The period is sometimes described as the "invisible revolution" or the "happy France", quite a positive reference!

The expression was actually first used by the French demographer Jean Fourastie in 1979 and the term is derived from "Les Trois Glorieuses", the three days of revolution from 27–29 July 1830.

The legacy of these fascinating post-war cultural, social and economic achievements has been an inspiration to many and explains several aspects of modern French society.

2. Discover French pop culture

In the art sphere, this prolific period saw the birth of minimalism and the French "Nouveau Realisme" which is the equivalent of English Pop Art. Many famous artists-to-be (Rancillac, Saint Phalle Arman, Fromanger, Dufrene, etc.) actually got most of their inspiration from advertising and mass consumption (finally a powerful creative trigger), and we bet you would be surprised by their audacious creations!

In fact, this period coincides with the emergence of the first family holidays in the 50s (think "Club Med"), the development of television and the boom of many new creative areas such as video advertising in the 60s. The first French supermarket opened in the 70s and many technological innovations set the tone of the future: the opening of the national aerospace centre in the 60s leading to the Ariane spaceship, the invention of the Concorde (the only commercial supersonic plane that ever flew), the Minitel, which was the first widely adopted computer network (then used by over 25 million French households), and so many more.

We will come back to a few surprising facts about these times later on, stay tuned!

Last, but not least, many cultural shifts took place and the popularisation of the mini skirt was just one of them...

THE LITTLE FRENCH BOX
#Minitel

A 1980s classic telephone, now seen as the ultimate beige plastic kitsch, is well-known as the "Little French Box". But what is less well-known is that it once was an audacious precursor of the World Wide Web and had a user-friendly design.

1. France Telecom was once innovative

The "Minitel" was invented in the 1970s when the state company France Telecom (now private and rebranded as the company Orange) came up with a system combining the telephone and information technologies: what the TGV was to train travel, the Pompidou Centre to art, and the Ariane project to rocketry, the Minitel was to the world of telecommunications. Other countries looked on in awe and admiration, and the French were proud.

At the height of its glory in the mid-nineties, 10 million households owned a Minitel device (distributed for free by the government), with over 25 million users (over 40% of the French population) connecting monthly to more than 23,000 services, free or paid per-minute on the phone bill. Yes, it was a national internet before the internet!

2. Dial "36 15"

Technology wasn't the same though: people had to dial-up a number with their old analogue box in order to connect their box to the network. The most common dial number was 36 15, followed by the name of a service. The French quickly used it to consult the yellow pages, check exam results, apply to university or book trains, years before the Silicon Valley was born. The most lucrative service turned out to be the first cybersex chat – the so-called Minitel Rose (Pink Minitel) – which made a fortune for a number of entrepreneurs such as Xavier Niel, now one of the wealthiest people in France! Every French person remembers 3615 Ulla.

3. Decline of an iconic symbol

Its biggest failure, however, was its inability to be exported abroad (and probably also its lack of innovation). A few attempts to spread the beige box were nevertheless carried out in a couple of countries, such as Greece, Belgium, the Ivory Coast and Japan, but the French never put any effort to support the roll-out of outsiders, confirming their national trait of self-centredness.

11

The Minitel was a uniquely French institution, eventually overtaken in the late 1990s by the World Wide Web and permanently closed down in June 2012.

A HINT OF FOREIGN SCENERY WITH A DOUBLE SHOT OF VIOLENCE AND SEX?

#Spy

1. Meet the most prolific French writer who ever existed

In his office, the walls are covered by assault rifles AK-47, erotic illustrations and pictures of African war lords.

Gérard de Villiers is the French writer who sold the highest number of books in the world. In 1964, an editor told him that Ian Fleming had just died: "you should take over". The first "SAS" came out a few months later. Because James Bond was English and because a Frenchman would not have been taken seriously, the hero is Austrian: "Son Altesse Sérénissime" (His Serene Highness), alias SAS, aka Malko Linge, an aristocrat freelancing for the CIA. Why the CIA? "There have only been two great intelligence services, the CIA and the KGB, in terms of resources and global reach", de Villiers explained, "France has good services, but they're limited." The hero was inspired by three real-life acquaintances: a high-ranking French intelligence official named Yvan de Lignières, an Austrian arms dealer, and a German baron named Dieter von Malsen-Ponickau.

"SAS" became the longest-running fiction series ever written by a single author. With 4 to 5 books a year, De Villiers wrote for 50 years until his death in 2013 at the age of 83. Traveling the world, his routine usually involved a trip of 15 days followed by 6 weeks of writing with "a hint of foreign scenery with a double shot of violence and sex". He finally wrote 200 books and sold around 150 million copies worldwide, ranking the series among the top 10 best-selling stories of human history!

De Villiers' books are well known for their in-depth insider knowledge of espionage, geopolitics, terrorist threats, as well as graphic sex scenes (when *The New York Times* suggested that the sex in SAS was unusually hard-core, he replied "maybe for an American, not in France.")

But there is more to it...

2. Connection with secret services around the world

Unlike most paperbacks, SAS attracted the attention of most intelligence officers and diplomats in the world. As de Villiers says, "my books are investigations describing real facts".

In the early seventies, de Villiers met the legendary Alexandre de Marenches, who led the French foreign-intelligence service for more than a decade. Their friendship deepened and so did his ties with French intelligence. "The French elite pretend not to read him, but they all do", said Hubert Védrine, the former foreign minister of France, who once told de Villiers over lunch: "I wanted to talk because I've found out you and I have the same sources". French Presidents Valéry Giscard and Jacques Chirac were unapologetic fans.

In fact, his books were ahead of the news. He even anticipated tumultuous events in a prophetic way, including the assassinations of Anwar Sadat, Gandhi, the American ambassador in Libya, the attack of the Syrian regime's command centres, and others.

He wasn't friends only with the French, but with top intelligence officers from around the world. Alla Shevelkina, a journalist who was his fixer on a number of Russian trips, said: "he gets interviews that no one else gets, not journalists, no one". A former CIA operative explained "I recommend our analysts to read his books, because there's a lot of real information in there. He's tuned into all the security services, and he knows all the players. There are even ministers from other countries who meet with him when they pass through Paris."

And if you wonder why these people divulge so much to a pulp novelist? De Villiers would reply: "they always have a motive. They want the information to go out. And they know a lot of people read my books, all the intelligence agencies." And when de Villiers describes intelligence people in his books, everybody in the business knows exactly who he's talking about, which is also exciting to them, especially as he never reveals their real names. Or almost never, as he forgot once to replace the name of the CIA station chief in Mauritania: the CIA was very angry, but his friends at the DGSE (the French foreign intelligence agency) apologised on his behalf.

HOW TO REACH FAME WITH ONE COLOUR ONLY: MEET YVES KLEIN

#Pop-Art #Blue

1. The first monochrome artist

There are the surprising reasons for why, alongside works by Andy Warhol and Willem de Kooning, Klein's paintings were among the top five sellers at Christie's Post-War and Contemporary Art sales at the beginning of the twenty-first century, some selling for over $35 million.

It all started in 1955 with an exhibition of a series of multicolour monochromes, which after being misunderstood by the public, led the French artist, at 29 years old, to his next show in 1957, featuring eleven identical blue canvases using ultramarine pigment, reminiscent of lapis lazuli.

Yves Klein was obsessed with the idea that pure colour means something in itself and he chose blue as the most abstract, stating "blue has no dimension and promotes imagination". The recipe was protected to maintain the "authenticity of the pure idea, the most perfect expression of blue" and was to become famous as "International Klein Blue" (IKB).

From then onward, this blue was to become an art: Yves Klein's Art. He dedicated the rest of his artistic life to this colour, through different mediums, and became known as "Yves the Monochrome".
At his next exhibition, *The Void*, Klein removed everything in the gallery, painted every surface white and then staged an elaborate entrance procedure for the opening night: the gallery's window was painted blue and a blue curtain was hung in the entrance lobby, accompanied by republican guards and blue cocktails.

An artistic myth was born.

2. Pioneer of performance art

If, to mark the opening of the "blue era", a thousand and one blue balloons were released and blue postcards were sent out (an act baptised as "aerostatic sculpture"), the real deal came few years later with a type of work he called "*Anthropometry*".

Imagine the maestro, Yves, in his Parisian gallery surrounded by a silent, shocked and excited audience, commanding a few naked women covered in blue paint to roll over and press themselves upon canvases, using the models

as "living brushes" to create new paints. Highly controversial, the first public experimentation would lead to a number of other performance works.
They were later enhanced with the audience dressed in formal evening attire while an instrumental ensemble of nine musicians played Klein's *The Monotone Symphony* (a single 20-minute sustained chord followed by a 20-minute silence). Klein's ideas were extravagant and radical at the time. What Allan Kaprow did in America, Yves Klein initiated in Europe: "happenings" were born. Artists such as Marina Abramovic praised Klein as the genius father of the performance art movement.

3. New Realism: the forerunner of French pop art

The "New Realism" movement was founded in Yves Klein's apartment in 1960 with other famous French artists such as painter Martial Raysse, poet Francois Dufrene, and sculptors Cesar, Gerard Deschamps, Nikki de Saint Phalle to name a few. It started with a manifesto where Yves Klein declares — "At present, I am particularly excited by 'bad taste'. I have the deep feeling that there exists in the very essence of bad taste a power capable of creating those things situated far beyond what is traditionally termed 'art' -

The New Realist Artists made extensive use of collage and assemblage, using real objects incorporated directly into the work and criticising mass-produced commercial objects (e.g., Jacques Villegle's ripped cinema posters, Arman's collections of detritus and trash).

Klein later appropriated famous sculptures, such as the Venus de Milo, by painting plaster casts of them with International Klein Blue. In 1958, he planned to use the Place de la Concorde in Paris by shining blue spotlights onto the central obelisk. The project was called *Blue Obelisk* but it was only realised in 1983, after his death.

DID YOU KNOW ABOUT 'SABERING' THE CHAMPAGNE?
#Champagne

The French not only behead their kings, but their bottles of champagne too! While cutting off heads has become politically incorrect, slicing off the collar and cork of a sparkling bottle is still tolerated. It unleashes the hidden sadistic side of every French gentleman, whilst displaying virile and cocky (yet sophisticated) manners to amuse guests and impress wives.

1. An unclear historical truth

Version 1: the forgotten version, aka the pretentious one
Napoleon loved champagne and never went to battle without a cart fully loaded: "in victory one deserves it; in defeat one needs it". In 1812, after kicking the ass of the Russians in Smolensk, the French officers got their share and used their swords to open the bottles. That was a bit premature as the Berezina was around the corner (oops).

Version 2: the impossible version, aka the foreign one
Some say the Cossacks did actually confiscate the stocks of the Emperor and humiliated the prisoners by breaking all the bottles before drinking them, in an attempt to destroy French traditions. None of the French believe this controversial story.

Version 3: the official version, aka the romantic one
Napoleon was a brilliant general, winning countless fights, territories and lands. He and his officers always celebrated in style, drinking at the vineyard of Madame Clicquot, who had inherited her husband's small Champagne house at the age of 27. The officers used to open their bottles with their sword to impress the rich, young and sexy widow. Absolutely, this is the way to go!

2. An ancestral (yet easy) technique

A champagne bottle holds a considerable amount of pressure. This is ideal to send the top flying upon opening. At the intersection of the seam and the lip lies a weak point: this is where the impact of the blade creates a crack that rapidly propagates through the glass, sending the collar flying in a demonstrative operation. Simple.

Beware, this may not be appropriate in a restaurant, in front of your fiancée or near your new TV. Depending on the situation, that can be a credible excuse to send your mother in law home for a few months or involuntarily damage the car of your favourite neighbour (hint: the target should not be more than 10 metres away). PS: the author denies all responsibility in case of unfortunate attempts.

Finally, the Order of the Golden Sabre (an international fraternity founded in 1986) would recommend using a champagne sword ("sabre à champagne"). That will cost you between £100 to £15,000 and does not guarantee that you will break the world record of 50 bottles opened in 60 seconds. It may also be slightly over the top: a simple and heavy kitchen knife will do.

IF "KISSING FANNY" SOUNDS POETIC TO YOU, YOU'D BETTER LEARN ABOUT THIS FRENCH HUMILIATION!

#Pétanque

1. "Kissing Fanny" (or "taking a Fanny") isn't a reward but a punishment!

If a French person asks you to kiss Fanny, don't get excited: you have probably been beaten somehow and are expected to pay the penalty!

This French tradition is said to originate from Lyon, where a young 20 year old lady named Fanny worked as a waitress in a bar of the Croix-Rousse neighbourhood. This kind hearted person used to show her butt to comfort the losers of a well-known French ball game, pétanque.

The local salacious French took great pleasure to repeatedly humiliate any team facing a serious defeat: from now on, anyone losing 13–0 would kiss the ass of this generous girl! The custom spread, and because it was not easy to find an open-minded girl like Fanny, she was substituted by a painting or sculpture of a generous rump. A tradition was born and every serious pétanque club now honours it!

2. The inspiring game behind is called "pétanque"

This traditional French sport was referred in the Middle Ages to as the "asgloblorum" game and was known as "boules" (i.e., "balls"), played throughout Europe. The game evolved into the "provençal game" in the south of France and the modern version was invented in 1910 by Ernest Pitiot, a local café owner of La Ciotat. Since then, it became "pétanque", deriving from the expression pès tancats meaning "feet planted" (on the ground)!

Two teams of two or three players alternatively throw steel balls (or "boules") of 1kg as near as possible of a smaller wooden one (the "cochonnet" or piglet in English, aka the "jack") in order to score points. The team that does not have the boule closest to the cochonnet continues to throw boules until it either lands one closer than their opponents or runs out of boules. You keep playing rounds until one of the teams reaches the score of 13. Easy isn't it? Last, if you don't want to "mark", by throwing a boule as close as possible to the jack, you can "shoot" the opponents' boules away from it. Et voilà!

3. Want to try?

The game spread to the rest of France, Europe, and then countries around the globe. On an international level, the governing body of pétanque is the Fédération Internationale de Pétanque et Jeu Provençal (FIPJP), which was founded in 1958 in Marseille. It has about 600,000 members in 52 countries, is responsible for organising a yearly world tournament and is lobbying the Olympic Committee to include this sport at the 2024 Games!

Who knows, maybe you'll discover a new passion, and become the new François De Souza, the iconic French triple world champion from the sixties!

DISCOVER THE SURPRISING LOVE AFFAIR BETWEEN THE VATICAN AND FRENCH WINE

#Wine #Sin

The Vatican consumes more wine than any other country: almost 100 bottles per person per year, nearly two times more than the alcoholic French (the second in the world, at 44 litres per person per year), and far ahead of timid Brits, who drink only 20 litres a year: who would have known that a few hundred Catholic priests would knock the English out in less than a round?

1. Is it the holy wine?

While your first thought may be that the ceremonial communion wine must account for some of this extravagant total, this is not so: sacramental wine is not usually bought off the shelf, since it needs to be made from pure grapes and cannot be mixed with other substances (according to the Code of Canon Law), hence this beverage is definitely not counted in the statistics.

2. So what? Is Vatican a place of debauchery?

During the "Renaissance", the Vatican was actually a place of sinners, according to Gaetano Moroni, hairdresser of pope Gregory XVI (1831–1846). It was a place to be avoided, where wine was poisoning spiritual souls. "Vaticana bibis, bibis venenum" (the Vatican drinks, it drinks poison) was already being written by the poet Martiale during the first century. With less than a dozen women for 800 old men with no children, life might have been tough behind those walls. The Italian cardinals and others churchmen may have found that a convenient alcoholic substitute is the perfect candidate to have a fling with. If you wonder why, ask the French: after all, they invented wine, love and "4-to-5" (the hour when you meet your lover in the afternoon)!

But could this be enough for such an addiction, or is there more to it?

3. Satanic money!

Since 1929, Italy has recognised the Holy See's full ownership and jurisdiction of Vatican City. Paul VI created at the time a sort of Finance Minister responsible for dealing with all its economic affairs and the IOR (Instituto per le Opere di Religione), aka the bank of the Vatican, an opaque (but convenient) structure that happens to own "lo spaccio dell'Annona" : the only local supermarket. It is a popular shop, indeed, where all the products are VAT and income free (thanks Mussolini for his the past favours)!

It's no wonder why all the accredited people, their friends, the friends of their friends, and a few clever smugglers spend some profitable times shopping there: the Holy See is in fact a giant duty-free shop! "Money is solely the excrement of Satan", the Italian Prime Minister Romano Prodi once said in front of many clerical representatives. "Of course, but the excrement of Satan can be used to fatten the fields of God", answered a fat prelate.

GAULOISE OR GITANE? A FRENCH SMOKING GUILTY PLEASURE
#Cigarettes

1. The birth of two iconic French brands

In 1910, one hundred years after Napoleon decided that tobacco was going to be a state monopoly, the former French state company SEITA (Société d'exploitation industrielle des tabacs et des allumettes) introduced Gauloises and Gitanes, two iconic brands of French cigarettes.

Both brands promoted their Caporal version, rolled with a brown tobacco which was originally distributed to corporals and of better quality than the type given to troops. Since Louis XIV, this type of tobacco was given for free to the French soldiers to boost their morale during armed conflicts, and between the World Wars, smoking Gauloises or Gitanes in France was considered patriotic and affiliated with French "heartland" values.

Development investments from SEITA initially focused on Gauloises as the brand was associated with the cigarette-smoking "poilu" (slang word for the French infantryman in the trenches) and the resistance fighters with the slogan "Liberté toujours" (Freedom always). The objective was also to replace the "Élégantes" cigarettes, which were more popular and cheaper, but less profitable. This was a winning strategy, as Élégantes disappeared in the fifties.

In the meantime, the classic Gitanes achieved a distinctive bit by using a special method of curing the tobacco. The result was a cigarette which was both strong in flavour and had a distinctive aroma. They would soon take over the French market with clever artistic branding.

2. Gitanes' winning strategy: a long history of collaboration with renowned artists

After famous designer Maurice Giot created an art deco-style pack design for Gitanes cigarette packets, the cigarette brand's continuous association with art and literature became trendy and kept boosting its appeal.

An image of a Gypsy dancer first appeared on Gitanes (which means 'gypsy women' in French) cigarette packets in 1943, designed by Molusson. In 1947, Max Ponty added a wisp of smoke. The dancer silhouette has been reworked by many famous poster designers, such as Savignac and Morvan. Such associations greatly increased brand awareness and created a powerful, upmarket identity, a quintessentially French design with a particular, cool allure!

The brand also benefited from considerable marketing investment over the years with over fifteen advertising campaigns between 1951 and 1976 and the efforts worked: French cigarette consumption during Les Trente Glorieuses consistently shifted from Gauloises to Gitanes. Gitanes moved from an entry level to a "superior" product, from a working class to a refined cigarette.

3. Want to be as cool as a rock star or philosopher? Smoke a Gitane!

The success of Gitanes not only relied on advertising and innovative design, but benefited from the power of world-famous artist endorsements! Writers, singers, actors, musicians – countless celebrities did choose to associate their personal brand with Gitanes: Albert Camus, Jean-Paul Sartre, Alain Delon, Jean Gabin, Johnny Hallyday, and the famous French five-pack-a-day chain-smoker Serge Gainsbourg, who once sang an anthem to the habit, entitled "God smokes". But international rock stars smoked them too: John Lennon (in an effort to deepen his voice), David Bowie (a big fan), Jim Morrison, and Paul Weller, who posed slipping a pack into his jacket pocket for the cover of The Face!

In 2008, these two iconic French brands were bought by Imperial Tobacco, a British company headquartered in Bristol and fourth-largest tobacco producer in the world! Who would have guessed the Brits would be seduced by the French glamour and "laissez faire"?

"ENJOY WITHOUT HINDRANCE": WHAT YOU DON'T KNOW ABOUT MAY '68

#History

Here is what really happened and the how-to recipe for driving big changes! May '68 wasn't only about sexual emancipation, weird hedonistic demands or freedom of speech, but was the biggest French social movement of the twentieth century, a massive spontaneous revolt against authority and capitalism, leading to a global social, cultural and political movement.

1. Chronology of an escalation

On Friday 3 May 1968, the Sorbonne, the prestigious university, was occupied by 400 teenagers in opposition to the rigidity of institutions (Church, schools, companies, and the political system) and who declaimed the "liberalisation of morals". At the time, the majority of schools weren't mixed, girls couldn't wear trousers, students couldn't smoke and young people faced authoritative paternalism. The police intervention led to a protest gathering of over 10,000 students on the night of 10 May in the Latin Quarter of Paris, with a dozen barricades erected and violent police repression. Trade unions consequently called for a solidarity protest.

On Monday 13 May, a massive demonstration (one million people) was organised by the leading workers organisation (CFDT) wishing to take control of the spontaneous movement. To the surprise of the general public, a massive strike started and spread quickly during the following days: it was the first global impulsive modern strike in a Western country where mass consumption was already in place.

Protests continued and the country was paralysed. Political leaders started to take advantage of the situation. The Grenelle Agreements, negotiated by Prime Minister Pompidou, the trade unions and employers, aimed at guaranteeing new social benefits but the discontent was still growing and De Gaulle dissolved the Parliament on 30 May.

The June elections crushed the movement, with an overwhelming victory for the right, but the political failure of the movement didn't prevent social and cultural progress. Many demands progressive demands were subsequently adopted: the decriminalisation of abortion, the end of censorship, the legal majority age lowered to 18, the liberalisation of the audio-visual industry, and so on.

2. Cultural impact

Although the events turned violent, they also exhibited artistic aspects, with multiple improvised debates, songs, imaginative graffiti and posters that inspired future generations.

Writing slogans on the walls of streets and universities became an extremely popular activity. The archives collected over 500 unique tags such as: "we are free to be free", "Be realistic, ask the impossible", "it is forbidden to forbid", and "enjoy without hindrance".

The explosion of public messages led to the creation of monthly paper Action (created to relay the claims from students, started in May 1968 and stopped in June 1969) and the organisation of public debate (The Odéon theatre was used as a free space to talk about the democratisation of culture). In Paris, the School of Fine Arts and the School of Decorative Arts became the "popular workshop", producing hundreds of designs and thousands of hand silkscreened posters between May and June 1968.

All these new public ideas remained in the collective memory and some brands later leveraged this for their advertising campaigns (e.g., Citroen for its car in 1994, and Leclerc for its prices in 2005).

Publicist Gilles Masson said: "we are in a society of nostalgia and reclamation. The scenery of contestation is well appreciated for its playful side and its fighting values". The irony is that using May '68 imagery obviously goes against the original spirit of the movement, which condemned mass consumption and capitalism.

MEET THE FRENCHMAN WHO EARNS OVER €1M PER HOUR
#LVMH

1. "I've got no email" says the richest man in France

It may sound old school and a bit odd, but apparently "just a phone" is enough to build an empire. Well... that and a small inheritance to start with: his daddy's civil engineering company that he took over in the late seventies.

Our man is obviously not in the digital scene, but is still an engineer. While American high society sends its heirs to Harvard Business School – and the Brits send theirs to Oxbridge – the French do actually prefer the scientific way. If you want to make money in France, you'd better like mathematics and join the elitist school, the École Polytechnique, as did almost half of the CEOs of the "CAC40" (the leading French stock market index that lists the 40 biggest French firms by value). So too did our man, who loves numbers for sure.

Don't picture a friendly geek. He is not a cold man, but he doesn't smile very much, prefers to operate in the shadows and avoids the spotlight. His entourage unanimously describes him as a sharp competitor and he concedes: "What I love is to win. What I love is being number one". It's probably true. After all, with over £40bn in his pockets, he ranks among the top 10 wealthiest people in the world and his conglomerate owns more than 70 successful brands. What is his secret?

2. The combination of instinct and concrete facts

As Bernard Arnault says, "it's imperative that both play a part: instinct is a dangerous thing and basing things solely on facts rarely works. You have to be just as mistrustful of straightforward rationality in business as you do of a uniquely gut approach".

And here we are: over the past eleven years, the market value of his group has increased eleven times and in 2015 his business revenues rose 20% while its profits rose 15%. His strategy has been consistent: acquiring or developing a portfolio of companies, run independently, in a decentralised way, where the strongest brands help finance those that are still developing. There has been only one focus: a long-term vision of things. It seems easy.

In a nutshell, he quickly liquidated his father's company and entered the glamourous sector of luxury when he bought Christian Dior in the early eighties. A few years later, he took control of Moet Hennessy and Louis

Vuitton: LVMH was born in 1987. Welcome to the world of Bernard Arnault and his "70 Maisons" (describing each of his brands). And just to make you dream, here they are:

- **Wine and Spirits***:* 24 Maisons (e.g., Moet, Veuve Clicquot, Hennessy, Ruinard, Belvedere, Dom Perignon)
- **Fashion**: 15 Maisons (e.g., Louis Vuitton, Berlutti, Christian Dior, Givenchy, Kenzo, Thomas Pink)
- **Perfumes and Cosmetics**: 10 Maisons (e.g., Guerlain, Aqua Di Parma, Loewe)
- **Watches and Jewelry**: 7 Maisons (e.g., Tag Heuer, Hublot, Bulgari, Zenith)
- **Distribution**: 6 Maisons (e.g., Sephora, Bon Marche)
- **Others**: 9 Maisons (e.g., Les Echos, Jardin d'Acclimatation)

The last word will be from the lovely Madame Benard, one of the corporate directors: "LVMH is so beautiful that it transcends the beauty of nature". Really? Damn, I almost cried!

DOES ABSINTHE REALLY MAKE PEOPLE MAD?
#Absinthe

1. Absinthe isn't normal alcohol, but a hallucinogenic one!

A critic once said: "Absinthe makes you crazy … It makes a ferocious beast of man, a martyr of woman, and a degenerate of the infant, it … threatens the future of the country". The special effect of drinking absinthe actually led to the term absinthism to draw a distinction from alcoholism! The natural chemical thujone (a compound of the wormwood ingredient, with an active structure similar to that of cannabis, THC) has been blamed for its alleged impact and classified the drink as an addictive psychoactive drug and hallucinogen.

The first to establish the rapid hallucinations of absinthe was the famous French psychiatrist Valentin Magnan, backed by many bohemian artists and writers of the time. Van Gogh's love affair with absinthe is considered to be the most famed in history, but the devotee Oscar Wilde describes its effect best: "After the first glass of absinthe you see things as you wish they were. After the second, you see things as they are not. Finally, you see things as they really are, and that is the most horrible thing in the world". Others describe it as a mind-opening experience with a "clear-headed" feeling of inebriation and of "lucid drunkenness". We can now understand why the drink was banned in France, the US and most of European countries at the beginning of the twentieth century!

2. Where does this "Green Fairy" comes from?

The love affair drinkers had with it gave it the nickname "La Fée Verte" (The Green Fairy) as it became a muse (but later became the Green Curse, when it was banned). Absinthe isn't only an anise-flavoured spirit extract derived from the "Holy Trinity" of green anise, sweet fennel, and leaves of "grand wormwood", but one of the most potent alcoholic drinks available, bottled at or above 70%. Created by Dr Pierre Ordinaire, a French doctor, the formula was later acquired by Henry-Louis Pernod in 1805 who built a large distillery in Pontarlier, France, under the new company name Maison Pernod Fils, now the second biggest spirit brand in the world.

The custom of drinking absinthe became so popular in bars, bistros, cafes and cabarets that by the 1860s, 5pm had become known as "l'heure verte", or "the green hour", the starting point of a flow of emerald absinthe into the later hours of the evening. Just before the ban, absinthe was the leading alcohol consumed in France, far ahead wine or any other liquors, at 36 million litres per year!

3. What is the "French Method"?

The traditional French preparation involves placing a sugar cube on top of a special slotted spoon above a glass filled with a measure of absinthe. Iced water is poured over the cube to slowly distribute the water into the absinthe: the final solution (1 part absinthe for 3–5 parts water) results in a milky opalescent liquid with dissolved essences and blossoming flavours! This is the oldest and purest method.

Perhaps because Brits only drink beers, absinthe was never banned in the UK, and a few bars in London have it displayed on their menu. You will hopefully find the original Pernod recipe, even if we have heard that the Mansinthe (a brand created by the American musician Marilyn Manson) recently won a Gold Medal in a spirit competition! It's definitely a drink for the naughty, but we know everyone has a mischievous side: you should give it a try.

SOMMELIER, POET AND FOOL
#Wine

1. Wine and lyricism

If you know everything about wine and food pairing, you may be thinking to qualify as a wine steward or getting the prestigious title of "sommelier" to work in a fine restaurant: a highly strategic role, on a par with the executive chef. But never believe it's just about serving booze or the Union of French Sommeliers may take you to tribunal! They are what I call true passionate professionals and their association website is quite lyric, somewhat peculiar and truly amusing.

Here is how they officially define themselves: "a sommelier is a man of relationships, loving people, master of himself, knowing how to repress his mood swings, masking fatigue and worries. Attentive, listening to others, accurate in his technical moves, fast, organised, vigilant, sober". It then becomes better, with a delicious "Kiplingesque" conclusion: "his encyclopaedic and technical knowledge must serve the customer, not the glory and the vanity of the wine man he is. Here is revealed its passion, its intellectual richness, its vinous culture, its organoleptic sensitivity. Fleeting moment but without which no one would like to do this job … If you know all this without becoming vain, arrogant and conceited, then, you will be a sommelier, my son!"

You're thinking, tough criteria? Wait! You will still need to wait ten years with relevant experience to attempt to attain the qualification of "master sommelier"! Then and only then, you may be ready to compete for the ultimate titles: best sommelier of your country and of the world!

2. World wine championship

It all started in the late sixties, when the Association de la Sommellerie Internationale (ASI) was created to federate other organisations in the world and promote the profession (53 countries and over 50,000 professionals are now members). Since then, they have organised the championship of the best sommelier of the world every three or four years, gathering over a thousand candidates each time.

It is not a surprise that half of the last 14 winners were French, starting with Armand Malkonian in 1969 to Olivier Poussier in 2000. The current one is the Swedish Jon Arvid Rosengren who won the title in front of a crowd of over 4000 people in Mendoza (Argentina) in 2016. So here is what you have to do:

First session: 90 min questionnaire about the history of wine, from the grapes to the product's geography, characteristics or production processes, followed by a 30min blind tasting of five wines and liquors and a 30 minute essay in a foreign language.

Second session: serving a jéroboam of champagne (this is a 5L bottle, bigger than the 3L magnum, in other word a strength test!), questions about association, food and drink, the decanting of a wine (removing the solid residues from the liquid) and another six wines blind tasting in 20 minutes.

Want to know the silly part? Among the twelve contenders in the final, the twelve best wine experts in the world, the blind tasting showed an immense gap of appreciation (!) with the same red wine not being distinguished between a Pinot noir from Bourgogne, a Cabernet Sauvignon from Bordeaux, a Grenache from the Rhone, an Italian Niebiolo, a Spanish Rioja or an Aleatico of Greece! At least I am not ashamed anymore, the best wine masters got it completely wrong too.

HOW A FRENCH MONK INSPIRED THE ENTIRE HIP HOP COMMUNITY

#Champagne

1. It all started with Benedict of Nursia

At the beginning of the sixth century, around 500AC, a lonely pious man started to think about a beautiful woman he had met in Rome. Facing desire, he took his clothes off and ... threw himself into a bush full of spines and nettles in order to become immune against future temptations. Well, that's quite radical, and not really "hip hop", isn't it? Hold on.

That actually impressed a few men at the time and they gave him the status of "Saint Benedict": a couple of hundred years later the Benedictine order had gathered thousands of monks! In 1636 Pierre was born in the Kingdom of France and became one of them, joining the Abbey of Hautvilliers. The ecclesiastic made the place flourish, doubling the size of its vineyard, and processing a new type of wine. It is probably for this reason that he received the most honorific title of "Dom", which comes from the latin word dominus meaning "master".

He was Dom Perignon, and invented champagne along with the scholar Dom Ruinart!

2. "Come quickly, I am drinking the stars!"

The legend attributes these words to Dom Perignon. There is likely no erotic allusion in this, but maybe only a call to his peers in exploring the potential of this beverage. His appeal was very well heard: shortly after, the widow ("veuve" in French) Nicole Clicquot (who inherited a domain from her husband) made the production at scale of the sparkling wine possible with a method called the "method champenoise". That was the starting point of a prolific period that saw the birth of many famous champagne houses such as Krug, Pommery, Bollinger, and many other brands emerging at the time!

Lesson learnt: I would dare to say "what starts with a carnal guilt can end up in a spiritual drink".

3. Powerful symbolism

50 million thin bubbles seem the best way to get drunk (according to the latest scientific research, bubbles help our various organs to absorb alcohol).

It is therefore not surprising that the bubbly got associated with celebrations, and became the mark of kings and aristocrats!

The art of champagne and royalty inspired the nineteenth century industry, and the form of the Champagne coupe glass was then modelled on the shape of Marie Antoinette's breast (adapted from a wax mould, of course). It was quite the symbol (even if your bubbly stays bubblier in a flute).

Champagne was on its way to becoming the ultimate luxurious party drink. It is by far a perfect ostentatious object to publicly demonstrate money, eroticism and power.

Now, what style of music promotes money and eroticism? Rap and hip-hop, indeed. Branson B. from Harlem is largely credited with introducing the drink to the likes of Notorious B.I.G. and Puff Daddy in the late eighties. They taught Americans about Moët; Jay Z and Dame Dash showed them Cristal: champagne became the currency of power in the rap scene.

It should therefore not come as a surprise to read various surveys unanimously ranking the hip-hop and rap community as the most significant consumers of champagne, drinking on average 30% more than the fans of any other music genre!

"By the mid-2000s, everyone was just champagned out", Director X says. "There was champagne in every video". If you still have some doubts, think about the bling aesthetic and how high-end champagne is prominently featured in rap videos. Now are you convinced?
So if you want to be a rapper, maybe you should seriously consider calling yourself "Dom something" but beware, French arrogance is still around the corner. In 2006 the president of Champagne Louis Roederer spoke about the attention rap stars brought to his brand: "What can we do? We can't forbid people from buying it." Jay-Z, offended, consequently bought the competition brand Armand de Brignac for a couple of millions and the sales of Roederer collapsed by 70% in the US during the following years (singing "I am a business, man").

HOW THE FRENCH NEW WAVE INSPIRED TARANTINO AND CO.

#Cinema

1. The emergence of the New Wave ("Nouvelle Vague")

Cinema is an art that shifted in the fifties. "It was in the process of becoming a new means of expression on the same level as painting and the novel" argued Francois Truffaut, one of the leaders of a French movement from the sixties, promoting iconoclasm through new shooting formats and social topics.

At the time, the group of French innovators gathered young critics from the newly born magazine *Les Cahiers du Cinema* (the oldest French paper on cinema), taking its rebellious roots from the cultural shift of Les Trente Glorieuses. They realised that French cinema was lacking an impactful identity and were looking to challenge the scene. As Rivette said: "I think that French cinema at the moment is unwittingly another version of British cinema. The films seem no more ambitious and of no more real value... British cinema is a cinema genre, but one where the genres have no genuine roots... It's a cinema based on the false notions of supply and demand. In trying to play by all the rules of the game they do it badly, without either honesty or talent".

Laying the groundwork for a set of new concepts, revolutionary at the time, writers became movie directors. Jean-Luc Godard, Francois Truffaut, Eric Rohmer, Claude Chabrol, Agnes Varda and few others would become more than a new generation of French filmmakers: they would represent a defining moment of innovation inspiring the entire industry.

The French "New Wave" was born, and became "neither a movement, nor a school, nor a group, but a quality".

2. What happened next?

The New Wave emphasized the importance of a national cinema and strongly criticised the traditional narrative flow of the time. The films integrated unprecedented methods of expression (such as long tracking shots) and were filled with irony or sarcasm. Part of their new techniques also portrayed characters with no obvious labels: protagonists no longer fell into set categories (in the classic sense). Some dialogues were improvised and movies were full of references, whether graphical, musical, literal, philosophical or historical, and also tended to refer to other films.

Truffaut, with *The 400 Blows* (Palme d'Or 1959), and Godard, with *Breathless*, met with unexpected international success, both critical and financial, which turned the world's attention toward the movement. It became a reference for many modern and forward-thinking filmmakers such as Martin Scorsese, Francis Ford Coppola, John Ford, Brian de Palma, Paul Schrader and others, who expressed their admiration about these French filmmakers and the influence they had on their artistic and production style.

Quentin Tarantino went a step further, dedicating *Reservoir Dogs* to Jean-Luc Godard and scripting the famous *Pulp Fiction* dance from Godard's movie *Bande à Part*, one of his biggest influence that actually led Tarantino to call his producing company "A Band Apart"!

3. Living legend Jean-Luc Godard

Jean-Luc Godard continues to push formal and aesthetic boundaries while pursuing his highly personal cinematic style. At 84, he won the Prix du Jury in Cannes in 2014 for his latest movie *Adieu au Langage*.

Godard is the mastermind behind one of the most iconic reference of the New Wave: *Breathless* (*À Bout de Souffle* in French). The movie (which won the Jean Vigo and best director awards in Berlin, 1960) is a rare, powerful and timeless film. This story, about a wandering criminal (young Jean-Paul Belmondo) and his American girlfriend, is definitely a must-see.

A DIVE INTO THE ABSURD FANTASY OF FRENCH ELITE!
#Absurd

Famous people can't be bored: they need distractions, or challenges if they consider themselves intellectuals (say writers). But what if they are French? Add a touch of extravagance and absurdity, et voilà, the recipe for the birth of Pataphysics and its subcommittees — a unique movement worth discovering!

1. Pataphysics: the core essence of the world

After French dramatist Alfred Jarry attained fame through the fictional exploits of anti-philosopher Dr Faustroll; the young writer Guillaume Apollinaire and painter Pablo Picasso elevated him to the rank of a fascinating heroic figure. His work led to "a branch of philosophy or science that examines imaginary phenomena; it is the science of imaginary solutions". Pataphysics grew into an official society in the sixties and saw the opening of the London Institute in 2000(!). So what's special about it? Everything: an amusing madness endorsed by eminent thinkers committed to useless pursuits and elaborated spoofs.
Insiders use, for instance, the most caricatural calendar ever invented: the pataphysical calendar, composed of 13 months (such as the month of "debraining", "phallus" or "Pshit") with new saints in the tradition of French anti-clerical humour. Today could be the "19 Haha 143" according to the calendar convertor (full calendar can be found online and fans of Isaac Asimov will love the saint of March 6).

Pataphysics influenced pop culture, literature (Boris Vian was a fan), cinema (Jean-Pierre Jeunet) or architecture (Le Corbusier) by exploring countless concepts through dozen of sub-committees, such as the "Glorious Protuberances" sub-committee (Max Ernst was an active member), the "Translations and Betrayal" sub-committee led by Barbara Wright or the "Sub-heard Moralities" sub-committee, to name a few.

2. OuLiPo: constraints make me free

One of the groups actually became quite famous and popular: l'Oulipo, which stands for "Ouvroir de litterature potentielle" (opener of potential literature) founded in 1960 by cynical novelist Raymond Queneau and mathematician Francois le Lionnais. L'Oulipo focuses on the invention and experimentation of literary "constraints" as powerful stimuli for imagination. They define themselves as "rats building their own labyrinth with the intent of escaping it".

Delirious constraints have been invented ever since (haï-kaïsation, eclipse, S+7, snowballs, and hundreds of fancy other ones). A famous "Oulipien" is French George Perec, with his masterpiece *La Disparition* (translated as *A Void*), a 300-page novel written without the letter "e", and an example of a lipogram. The American Harry Matthews is another Oulipien with his book *Singular Pleasures*, describing 61 different scenes, each told in a different style, in which 61 people of different ages, nationalities, and walks of life masturbate.

If you want to join, it may be difficult as there are only approximately 20 members, only appointed by endorsement from existing members: you can refuse, but once elected, only suicide (in front of a solicitor) allows you to resign. After a natural death, you remain a member with the status of "excused". However feel free to be an enthusiastic supporter and attend their monthly Thursday gathering at the National French Library in Paris.

The movement may be absurd, but so what? This is just an exquisite illustration of nonsense being a powerful creative driver: we told you, the French can be fun!

BD: THE "NINTH ART" AND ITS FESTIVAL
#Graphicnovels

1. The Explosion of Bandes Dessinées

While some ignoramus may think "Bandes Dessinées" (literally "drawn strips", aka "BD") are what comics are to the Americans or what Mangas are to the Japanese, the difference is very great. In the twentieth century, Bandes Dessinées became recognised as the "Ninth Art": not exclusively for the young, and not just frivolous, but proper graphic novels bringing the best artists and designers together across a variety of genres and styles, creating a new form of art.

The origin is Franco-Belgian. Before the sixties, newspapers published them targeting a young audience: think *Tintin* from Hergé or *Asterix* from Goscinny and Uderzo. However it quickly expanded to new horizons with a broad diversity of themes, an adult audience, hardcover format and blockbuster series, thanks to the emergence of new specialised publishing houses such as Casterman or Delcourt.

Their influence on society was so strong that BD would soon become a part of French identity and popular culture: every household has a BD collection, every school supports a BD club, most French corporations invest in a BD library and the market size is almost as big as traditional literature (but it's much more engaging, the fans would say).

2. Angoulême: the pinnacle

In the early seventies a festival born in Angoulême, France, saw an exponential growth. Nowadays it gathers 200,000 international visitors on average every year: this is the biggest and most prestigious event of its kind in the world. If you know the Cannes Festival (and who wouldn't?), you will enjoy its similarities the one in Angoulême. There is an official selection of 40 albums and a jury awarding the best album of the year with the "Fauve d'Or" prize. There is also the Prix Special and the Grand Prix given to an author to recognise career achievements. The winner of the Grand Prix actually becomes President of the Jury for the following year and designs the next official poster!

In the mid-eighties, Jack Lang, the French Minister of Culture, inaugurated a museum and research centre dedicated to Bandes Dessinées: the International City of Bandes Dessinées and Images! Yes, in France, this is big!

3. French stars and award winners

The best designers and artists in the profession are considered rock stars, with major commercial successes and strong influence on other areas such as cinema. Here is a selection:

- **The Incal**: a science fiction space opera by Moebius (a pseudonym) and Jodorowksi
- **The Seven Lives of the Sparrowhawk**: an historical intrigue during the seventeenth century in the Kingdom of France by Cothias and Julliard
- **XIII**: a political thriller by William Vance and Jean Van Hamme
- **Who Killed the Idiot?** : a dark humour tale by Dumontheuil
- **The Power of the Chninkel**: a one-shot black and white heroic fantasy story by Rosinski
- **Frustrated**: a humoristic satire of young adults by Claire Bretécher

WHY RICARD WON THE PASTIS WAR
#Pastis

1. Pernod vs Ricard

Pastis isn't only an anise-flavoured alcohol, it's a French national symbol born after the ban of absinthe a hundred years ago! The green fairy being illegal, the Pernod company had to quickly find a substitute: it leveraged its strong distribution network in the south of France to promote the new 45% drink in the twenties.

But Pernod was not counting on Paul Ricard, an aspiring painter from Marseille and son of a wine merchant who refused the family business to take up an artistic path. At age twelve, Paul met Mr Espanet, an old hairdresser who had a secret: a special recipe to produce the best pastis of the area, with fennel and licorice. Inspired, the teenager would devote all his time to develop his new passion: create the perfect "Pastaga".

In the thirties, the county of Provence went crazy about the drink and a 40-year war ensued: Pernod vs. Ricard, until they ultimately merged in the 70s, led by Ricard's heir. Here is the story of what happened.

2. Marketing mastering

Through business, the creativity of Ricard found new ways to blossom.

With the motto "the real pastis of Marseille", Ricard launched a genius marketing coup, linking the drink to the city and to his name. The brand "Ricard" was on its way to become the market standard and saw its popularity increase tenfold. At the bar, people now ordered "un Ricard". With his sensitivity for design, Paul developed himself all the collateral aspects, from the advertisement posters to the bottle's shape.

But the key innovation came from abroad. After the Second World War, Ricard took an eye-opening business trip to the US. At his return, he led his company to be the first French organisation to develop a new commercial tactic: sponsoring! Ricard took over this virgin area to push his advantage and the impact was enormous. In 1948, the caravan of the Tour de France had a complete make-over and was transformed in a yellow-blue Ricard rolling machine. At night, free gigs gathered the biggest upcoming and established stars (Charles Trenet, Annie Cordy, etc.), all promoting the brand, which was now the number one pastis producer in the country.

3. Revolutionary cherry on the cake

If this wasn't enough to convince you, the following story shows the visionary touch of the leader, who was described as "a benevolent capitalist" and could be one of the heroes of Les Trente Glorieuses, a sharp business mogul promoting social values and creating one of the strongest corporate cultures ever seen.

He understood that his employees must be his best allies, his ambassadors, and his devoted soldiers. What could achieve that best than offering them the best rights and benefits and creating a strong feeling of belonging? The structure Ricard created was more than a company, it became an enlightened entity providing free holidays for workers' families, support for accommodation, 30% higher wages than industry standard, lavish business trips for everyone in yachts and palaces, a pool of shares (these actually made Modeste Bovis, the personal assistant of Ricard, a multi-millionaire), and so on.

This is how Ricard became a legend.

Pernod-Ricard is currently the third largest spirit company in the world (behind Diageo and Bacardi), pastis is the number one spirit in France, and the dynasty is in good shape, with Alexandre Ricard, Paul Ricard's grandchild, leading the way! As we say in France, "un Ricard, sinon rien" (a Ricard, or nothing).

WE GIVE A FRENCH TOUCH TO HOUSE MUSIC
#Music

1. The genesis of French house music

The first French electronic music followers emerged in the early nineties amongst the gay community of Paris, regulars at La Luna or guests of the "mixed" nightclubs Le Rex and Le Palace, which threw the first couple of house music parties.

Techno music fan and artistic director at Barclay Records Eric Morand tried to promote the genre but faced contempt. He left Barclay's to start Fnac's Music Dance Division in 1991: "my boss at the time wasn't passionate but understood the trend. My main ambition was to launch French artists such as Ludovic Navarre (aka Saint Germain) and Laurent Garnier". The latter discovered house music in England, was influenced by the Detroit scene, and became a legendary pioneer, the first electronic artist to receive an award in France.

Still, very few customers were interested even if electronic events started to grow. A few singles of the label became hits in 1994, but despite these successes, Morand didn't feel supported anymore. He decided to create his own label, F Communications, with Garnier. They attracted all the local DJs of the time and invented a motto for French partygoers who liked house music: "We Give a French Touch to House".

The name was on its way to being established.

2. From iconic Radio FG to "Respect" parties

The early nineties also saw gay figure Henri Maurel take over Radio FG (98.2 FM). Trusting his new A&R head Patrick Rognant and a young team of DJs and journalists, the radio quickly became the official station of the underground scene, house music clubs and techno raves. The programmes *Rave Up* or *Happy Hour* (renamed *Global Techno*) aimed at popularising techno culture, and "not only artists were invited but event organisers, authors, and journalists". All the first international stars were there, at the decks or in interviews: Jeff Mills, Carl Cox, Derrick May, DJ Hell, Dave Clarke, Coldcut or Underground Resistance – and most of the key French Touch figures also passed by Radio FG's studios.

Journalist Jérôme Viger-Kohler helped the movement shine by creating the "Respect" parties in 1996 for the gay club Le Queen. They were looking for a new audience on Wednesdays. A free event was born, a gathering straight and gay, black and white, with very lax entrance criteria (a rare door policy in Paris) and a range of French DJs. It was a massive hit, surfing on the local funky groovy house.

3. The movement's explosion

The nascent French Touch movement started to attract more and more talent, artists playing with aesthetic references and recycling themes from past musical decades. DJ Cam produced sounds influenced by trip-hop with *La Vague Sensorielle*, Trankilou with *Atom Funk* and Motorbass with *Pansoul* brought warm funky resonances, Etienne de Crecy gathered the collective project *Super Discount* and new specialised French labels emerged (such as Yellowprod with its *Africanism* series). In 1998, the single *Music Sounds Better With You* from Stardust (Thomas Bangalter from Daft Punk, Benjamin Diamond and Alan Braxe) became emblematic and sold over two million copies worldwide in a few months.

French singles quickly started to top English charts and British music journalists started to use the expression "French Touch", contributing to the diffusion of this movement. The term was widely used for the first time by MTV UK during the Christmas holiday period of 1999 to describe the so-called "French house explosion" phenomenon. Bob Sinclair was interviewed, as well as Cassius. French musicians started to realise they could address the entire world: Dimitri from Paris, Martin Solveig, and many more would follow!

In the early 2000s, The Supermen Lovers created the sensational *Starlight,* topping the charts in UK and France, but the star was then Saint Germain: *Tourist*, mixing black, soul and jazz influences, selling over two million copies, and winning three Victoires de la Musique (the French Grammy Awards) and concluded with a triumphal tour of 200 dates. Oh, we almost forgot Daft Punk, most famous for their musical robots and their multiple hits *Da Funk*, *Around the World*, *One More Time* and many others.

Put simply, the French Touch legacy completely transformed the EDM industry!

PATHE AND GAUMONT: A SECRET LOVE STORY
#Cinema

Discover how the French movie industry is, in fact, controlled by only one family.

1. The two oldest film companies in the world

Gaumont (founded in 1895 by the engineer-turned-inventor Léon Gaumont) and Pathé (founded in 1896 by the Charles Pathé and his brothers) are respectively the first and second oldest still-operating film companies in the world, preceding Universal Studios and Paramount Pictures. They both led the world motion pictures scene for a while thanks to a range of innovations (e.g.: the newsreel and phonograph records) and acquisitions (e.g.: the Lumiere Brothers' patents).

While the Second World War impacted them, the global interest in the New Wave in the 1950s (as well as the nudity within French films) allowed their productions to successfully compete against American studios.

Their core activities now focus on cinema production and distribution with a catalogue of thousands of movies, including commercial hits such as the classics *Excursion to the Moon, Alfred Hitchcock, The 39 Steps, Ascenseur pour l'Échafaud* or more recently *Slumdog Millionaire, Bienvenue chez les Ch'ti* and *Intouchables* (which became the highest-grossing movie of all time in a language other than English, with a box-office of $361 million).

They also have majority stakes in several television networks across Europe (BskyB, for instance) and run one of the biggest cinema theatres chain in Europe, with over 1000 screens, through a joint venture called "Cinemas Gaumont Pathé": they basically dominating the EU market and so have no issues being in bed with each other.

This is indeed a family affair.

2. The Seydoux empire

In 1975, media tycoon and French multi-millionaire Nicolas Seydoux started managing Gaumont: he personally owned 60% of the shares and 70% of the votes. In 1990, Jérome Seydoux, then head of conglomerate Chargeurs, bought the company Pathé for 1bn French francs, becoming the new CEO.

Guess what? Nicolas and Jérome are brothers, the sons of Geneviève Schlumberger, heirs of the Schlumberger industrial oil dynasty but more inclined to shine on the red carpet. The new generation wouldn't deny: Léa (Seydoux Fornier de Clausonne), grand-daughter of Jérome, caught the public eye when she was picked by Quentin Tarantino for the opening scene of *Inglorious Bastards*, and when she was awarded the Palme d'Or at the Cannes Festival in 2013 for her role in *Blue is the Warmest Colour*.

It is helpful to belong to one of the top 50 wealthiest family of France with a fortune of several billion euros (and a couple of castles)…. but let's be grateful: they also created the largest database of French videos archive of the 20th century.

LAUGHTER IS PROPER FOR... COWS
#Food

Who doesn't know The Laughing Cow? Read here how this timeless French brand was born a century ago to mock the Germans, and why it finally conquered the world.

1. A special thanks to Richard Wagner

At the beginning she wasn't red, didn't wear earrings and was not even smiling. She had, however, a funny face: during World War I, this cow was the design put on every army train and vehicle providing meat to the troops. The drawing from illustrator Benjamin Rabier was selected after winning a national contest organised by the military. It was quickly nicknamed "Wachkyrie", a play of words making fun of the "Valkyries", the name of the Germans troop transports.

A few years later, Léon Bel, who was already running a successful family cheese business, remembered the joke: he patented the name "La Vache Qui Rit" ("The Laughing Cow") to brand his new soft cheese. Calling the original designer Rabier, they came up with a couple of twists, changing the original design into a new powerful logo. This was the birth of a new visual icon.

Few brands trigger so much sympathy and manage to be cross-generational: this friendly cow symbolises the warm feeding mother. The product is loved by children, who transmit this legacy when they become parents themselves. In other words, La Vache Qui Rit is a brand masterpiece!

2. Pioneering the art of marketing

Bel was one of the first businessmen to treat market analysis and advertising as key pillars of his company. These innovative practices (at the time) led to the round packaging and contributed to nailing down a specific communication (promoting the natural components of the product). The market studies would later bring many innovations, such as the infamous Apéricubes, born in the sixties!

Bel was also one of the first to understand the influencing power of children, and the benefits of promotional items. Millions were injected in goodies and sponsoring activities, then on radio and TV ads, up to the opening of a museum/theme park in 2009 in one of its former cheese factories!

Finally, the company quickly expanded abroad with a winning strategy: translating its name into the local language. It conquered 120 countries by the end of the century.

Now selling more than 10 million boxes a day, La Vache Qui Rit is one of the best French industrial successes of the twentieth century, marrying French elegance and humour to a cheeky cheese. Yummy, let's have some tonight!

THE SEXIEST HAND IN THE WORLD
#Water

1. The story started in a French spa

Once upon a time in the city of Vergèze, near sunny Montpellier, the domain des Bouillens, a disused spa, was sold to a doctor from Nimes. He made a discovery: the local water had mysterious properties. After teaming up with young English Sir John Harmsworth, he transformed the source into a commercial water production machine in 1906. 30 years later, the water was officially declared of "French public utility", was drank in Buckingham Palace, and was put in 19 million bottles annually. In the fifties, over 150 million bottles a year were produced, up to 120,000 per hour in the seventies. Accounting for 80% of the imported water in the US, it became the number one brand of mineral water in the world: this is the sparkling water Perrier, named after its founder!

2. And then, the scandal

Jean Davray, novelist and theatre writer emerged as the genius creative brain of the brand, introducing the famous motto "Perrier, it's mad". Moreover, the sparkling beverage became a prestigious product for the masses, a snobbish French water and soon a sassy, transgressive icon thanks to… a hand!
In 1976 the management asked young advertising agency Langelaan and Cerf to underline the offbeat twist of the drink. An ad was born… censored after it was shown but half a dozen times: it was too provocative and against morality! Nobody saw it but everybody talked about it. All the newspapers were headlined "Perrier, the scandal". The main character? The most famous hand on Earth that definitely helped associate the brand with pleasure.
And then, in 2009, the agency Olgilvy brought it back with a twist! A series of exclusive investigations were broadcast online, the first digital campaign of Perrier.

3. Are you ready to meet the sexiest hand in the world ?

In the late seventies, the Hand was a worldwide pop star, displayed on the front pages of the most prestigious publications and meeting the most influential personalities of the planet such as the president, Michael Jackson and the pope! But the Hand wasn't prepared to meet fame and quickly fell into drugs and decadence. Forgotten, abandoned by her friends, she tried to survive, accepting controversial roles and even being the lead actress of the infamous movie Striptease. The tribute recently paid by Ogilvy was more than welcome: we should never forget the major influence the Hand had on our French popular culture. Ready to see the original? Look on YouTube (you have been warned).

At least, advertisers were brave 40 years ago... who would dare, nowadays?

MEET DJANGO, FRENCH GYPSY ICON
#Jazz

1. A life of tragedy and virtuosity

A true French Tzigane "manouche" (gypsy), living in a caravan and moving from city to city, Django spent most of his youth in the poor and popular suburbs of Paris during the early 1900s. Uneducated and illiterate, his family only survived from music. Playing the violin first, banjo-guitar later, the young Jean gained his nickname "Django" meaning "I awake" at an early age.

A violent fire enflamed his caravan at age 18, leaving him badly injured and disabled with a leg almost amputated and two fingers paralysed. But the young virtuoso developed entire new guitar techniques that allowed him to transcend his infirmity and shape his own revolutionary style: the mark of a genius in the making! Generation of fans would push their devotion to the point of harming their fingers in an attempt of reproducing the art of their master.

While hundreds of thousands of Sinti Gypsies were deported and murdered by the Nazis during the Second World War, Django only survived because of the protection of surreptitiously jazz-loving Germans such as Luftwaffe officer Dietrich Schulz-Kohen, nicknamed "Doktor Jazz".

But despite his immense fame in the following years, alcohol and drugs made him miss sold-out concerts frequently and he developed a reputation of extreme unreliability, until his death at 43 from a brain tumour.

2. From the Hot Club de France onward

The innovative marriage of guitar and violin through his life partnership with another French legend, violinist Stéphane Grappelli, contributed to his attaining glory, especially after their band Quintette du Hot Club de France became a smash hit in Europe. This was the beginning of a historic success in the history of jazz music.

Django gained the admiration of the most famous musicians of the time as being an exceptional guitar player. The discovery of jazz came as a shock to him and he dedicated his life to the development of a new style combining jazz with his gypsy legacy, in a style that soon became known as swing manouche!

He not only performed with artists such as Duke Ellington, Benny Carter, Louis Armstrong, Adelaide Hall, and Dizzy Gillespie, but was amongst the few French musicians acclaimed in the US. He even received an outstanding six curtain calls on his first night at the Carnegie Hall in New York! The press was unanimous "possibly even in America there is no guitar player quite as 'hot' as Django".

3. Celebrating his legacy

The influence of Django went across time and genres; he became a major reference for the entire community of guitarists who all recognised his ground-breaking genius (did you know Jimi Hendrix named his album Band of Gypsys in his honour?).

Celebrated as an icon and hero in the gypsy world, tens of thousands of people still gather every year during the Django Festival, near Fontainebleau, France where he died: five days of amazing music at the end of June!

London also has a little gem, an intimate French brasserie dedicated to Django and his music, with live gigs all year long, the Quecumbar in Battersea is definitively a place to discover.

GOD SAVE FRANCE! SECULARISM AND SATIRE HISTORY
#Religion #JeSuisCharlie

After the *Charlie Hebdo* attack, a few words and tribute to French freedom of speech.

1. The tradition of secularism

We are lucky in France: joking about religion exposes us to terrorists but, at least, people are protected by the state (unlike the majority of the world). After heads were cut off during the Revolution, the clergy lost its privileges and society progressively affirmed the freedom of thought over religion. In 1905, church and state were officially split by law proclaiming a strong secular Republic, and its principles were incorporated into the French constitution in 1958: "the Republic protects freedom of consciousness. It guarantees the free practice of religions under the sole restriction of the public order interests".

It isn't about fighting religion but forbidding its influence on the political sphere. The state must be neutral and protect republican equality: no opinion is above another. Religious and anti-religious expressions are admitted: there are no offenses for proselytising or blasphemy; these are protected rights.

2. The birth of a "new secularism"

The growth of multi-culturalism and the diversity of religious practices, fuelled by immigration, the migrant crisis and a context of economic struggles has been generating debates in France around the concept of "national identity" and the need to clarify some religious rules in society.

The concept of "new secularism" emerged in the 2000s when the stakes of secularism shifted from the religious sphere to the cultural. It defined a common space not only run by a secular state but by a secular society, where religion should be constrained to the private/intimate realm. After almost a decade of preparation, it led to the creation in 2013 of the Laicity Observatory, a state organ aiming at proposing legal frameworks to assist the government in the defence of secularism: "in 1905, secularism was simply the separation of state and religions. Today a border has to be defined between the intimate, which must be protected, and the public, which must be preserved".

3. *Charlie Hebdo*, freedom of speech hero

The satirical magazine *Charlie Hebdo* was born during Les Trente Glorieuses, featuring cartoons, polemics and jokes forcefully defending feminism, ecology, and counter culture, condemning militarism, the extreme right and racism, and criticising religions (mainly Catholicism, but Islam and Judaism as well). It took its name after the death of General Charles de Gaulle and adopted the slogan "beastly and nasty" ("bête et méchant") that made entered everyday parlance in France. The "*Charlie* spirit" is about being able to laugh about anything, being controversial while keeping in mind its ideal of fighting for social justice and against extremism.

In 2006, *Charlie* published the Danish caricatures of Mohammed, which triggered violent reactions from some Muslim communities around the world: both Sarkozy and Hollande expressed their support for the ancient French tradition of satire.

In 2011 its office was fire-bombed following the publication of an edition entitled "Charia Hebdo", denouncing the post-election introduction of sharia law in Libya, the oppression of women, domestic violence, forced marriage and the stoning of those accused of adultery.

In January 2015, two Islamist gunmen forced their way into the headquarters and killed twelve employees of the magazine, including publishing director Charb, who had declared in the past:
"before being bothered by fundamentalist Muslims, we faced Catholics far right extremists. We mainly cover the Catholic Church and clergy because of its weight in France. The criticism is not of believers but of alienation in faith".

French in London could only notice how most UK media hypocritically censored *Charlie*'s covers "so as not to offend". At least France stands for an ideal of speech that must not be intimidated by violence, constraints, threats or state interests. That is why French people and people around the world adopted the slogan "Je suis Charlie".

A TASTE OF FRENCH MAGIC
#Beer

1. Hop farmers, new French stars?

Humble farmers from Alsace were recently furious. They felt insulted about being compared to British football players. France may indeed well be the only country celebrating its grangers, the land of opportunity for agriculture. Still, farmers refuse any suggestion that fame had gone to their heads, claiming that celebrity lifestyle doesn't interest them. "We cultivate hops because we love hops and the tasty beer they produce". They deny any relations with "kiss 'n' tell" bimbos, and claim they have "no interest in nightclubs" but acknowledge their luck (even if they have talent) to be paid for doing what they love. The controversy was born after a special investigation from Kronenbourg revealed the true sex appeal of French hop farmers.

2. A long French brewing history

Thousands of breweries have been running French beer history for decades. They developed the national culture with local atypical successes and massive worldwide hits, putting France in a peculiar quality position for beer connoisseurs!

Two regions have been leading the way. The turbulent Alsace-Lorraine, whose heart flirted for a while with Germany, is the main national beer production area with a flourishing number of breweries (some in place for centuries) in and around Strasbourg. The runner up is the Nord-Pas-de-Calais, sometimes called the "French Flanders" for its longstanding ties to Belgium, with whom it shares a common brewing heritage.

3. Giving birth to iconic drinks!

A couple of French beers made history; here are the unavoidable top four:

Kronenbourg 1664: the most sold French beer in the world and one of the market leaders for high-end premium beer is actually the fifth oldest beer brand in the world that still exists today! Founded in 1664 by Jerome Hatt, it was named after the location of Cronenbourg, on the hills above Strasbourg, where the brewery from the Hatt family moved in 1850. 1664 ale's golden highlights and delicate bitterness come from selecting the best hops, the "Strisselspalt". It has been a true French icon for over 350 years.

Pelforth: this became a strong specialty ale beer in the early twentieth century. Three brewers from Lille got inspired and created two different types of malt and English yeast. It was originally called Pelican, after a dance popular at the time, but the name was changed during Les Trente Glorieuses, merging "Pel" with "forte" (meaning "strong") and adding "h" at the end to give it an English feel: yes, British did have an influence there!

Desperados: this is a recent and cool Tequila-flavoured beer that took over the market in the late nineties to become one of the top 5 beers consumed in France! Young and sexy, it hit the sweet spot to be trendy! The brewer was "desperate" to find a name when he created it.

Tha…Wack: this is the world's best dark beer. It is an original young product created in a French pub in Paris, the Frog, which actually won the Gold medal award at the World Beer Awards in 2015!

So as you can see, not all that glitters is gold (nor champagne), it's also good old beer!

CREPES: A STORY OF LOVE, DRAMA AND BETRAYAL
#Crêpes

Crêpes (or "pancakes" in English) did unchain the passion of two famous chefs who fought for love and fame at the end of the nineteenth century. As usual, a woman was behind the conflict: Suzette. But who was she? Here is what we discovered after a thorough investigation from the kitchen of the Savoy Hotel in London.

1. For the love of Suzette

It all started with Monsieur Joseph, owner of Restaurant Marivaux, located in front of the Comédie-Française (a state theatre in Paris), who delivered a show in which a maid served crêpes on stage. Young and pretty French actress Suzanne Reichenberg, whose nickname was Suzette, was assigned to the task. Old and single Monsieur Joseph, inspired by his new muse, decided to flame the thin pancakes to impress the lovely girl. Despite the recipe's popularity with the audience, the young insolent girl kept declining the courtship of the cook, who then sneakily invited her for a training session.

While she was working on her pan, he viciously came from behind to satisfy his vice. His weakness of the flesh had two major impacts. Firstly, surprised Suzette jumped, accidentally throwing the crêpe up in the air: she later did it again on stage in a theatrical and aesthetic fashion, and like this, the tradition of "crêpe sauté" was made popular in France. Secondly, the old harasser decided to escape his trouble by immigrating to London, where he took charge of the kitchen of the Savoy Hotel whilst mourning his loss.

2. The fame of his name

A few years later, a talented and ambitious French chef, Auguste Escoffier, was becoming known among aristocrats, emperors and artists. Prince Edward recommended him to join the UK to help spread French refinement across the Channel. Mr Joseph was looking for a successor and naturally offered Escoffier to join the Savoy Hotel in 1890, teaching him all he knew and mentioning the recipe of the Crêpe Flambé with Grand Marnier.

When King Edward VII came to visit accompanied by a young lady also named Suzette, Joseph was away and Auguste took the opportunity to prepare the famous recipe. He later wrote in his diary:

"The King asked me the name of that which he had eaten with so much relish. I told him it was to be called Crêpe Princesse, which I just came up with; but he protested with mock ferocity because of the lady present. 'Will you', said His Majesty, 'change Crêpe Princesse to Crêpe Suzette?' Thus was born and baptised this confection."

Auguste of course never mentioned Joseph's influence, and did claim the ownership of the recipe, which contributed to his fame amongst the powerful. That probably helped him to become the first French chef to be awarded the Legion d'Honneur in 1919, a national distinction celebrating the most influential French figures.

3. The British legacy

Crêpes have been popular in France for centuries and especially in Brittany with its savoury buckwheat flour pancakes. Unfortunately, Crêpe Suzette's success didn't last in the UK, and typical French crêperies are rare, even in London. We can only recommend one: "La Petit Bretagne". After all British deserve a piece of this French dish, they contributed to its history!

FRENCH FRIED VACATION
#Cinema #Comedy

French comedy films went through a whole generation of actors and screenwriters who started in Parisian theatres, but one them had an unlikely impact on the modern French comedy landscape: Le Spendid!

1. 'Le Splendid' theatre

Cafconcs (an abbreviation of "café-concert") always proved popular in the capital. They were relatively small venues, but were ideal for performers to sing, play, dance or act whilst customers were having a drink. The "Casino Saint Martin" in the Fourth Arrondissement (borough) was just one of hundreds of spots in Paris until the cinema emerged. In the early fifties it became a movie theatre specialised in adult movies (!) until it went bust in the late seventies when a young band of friends saw an ad, discovered the place and decided to buy it! They renamed it after their collective's name: Le Splendid!

The group was born a few years earlier in the posh neighbourhood of Neuilly, where a team of childhood friends and aspiring actors started to write plays and comedies. Their names were soon to be linked to the most successful comic films of French cinema during the eighties and nineties. They all became loved stars and popular icons. Who are they? Christian Clavier (cast in *Les Visiteurs*, which was number one in 1993 and the fifth highest grossing movie in France), Michel Blanc (cast in *Grosse Fatigue*, which won the best screenplay in Cannes in 1994), Josiane Balasko (cast in *Gazon Maudit*, which won Cesar award for best director in 1995), Thierry L'Hermitte (cast in *Le Dîner de Cons*, which was second highest grossing at the box office in 1998, after *Titanic*) and Gérard Jugnot (cast member and director of *Meilleur Espoir Féminin*, which was nominated for most promising actress in 2001). But it was through two cult films that they reached fame in the early eighties: *Les Bronzés* (also known by its English title *French Fried Vacation*) and *Le Père Noël est une Ordure* (*Santa Claus is a Stinker*).

2. When will I see you again?

Both films first started on stage, where they got instant public recognition and sold millions of tickets during their initial theatrical releases.

Les Bronzés (which means, literally, "The Tanned") satirizes life at summer holiday resorts and depicts the adventures of a group of outrageous characters ranging from a clumsy dredge, a couple cheating on each other, a naive lady looking for love and many more. Its sequel portrays the same group spending a week's holiday at a ski resort. Popular, sarcastic and funny, the plots bring a spot-on critique of the type of vacation enjoyed by the French, with a playful twist.

Le Père Noël est une Ordure is a hilarious caricature of a trashy Christmas Eve shift in the Paris office of a telephone helpline for depressed people: no wonder it is played over and over by TC channels during Christmastime! These films quickly became legendary and endless lines passed into common speech, such as:

"You and me we have kind of the same issue, we can't rely on our looks, especially you, so forget that you have no chance and just give it a go. You never know, on a misunderstanding it may work"

If you want to impress your French friends, refer to one of these popular hits, and their engagement will be guaranteed.

TV, PUPPETS AND POLITICS: A FRENCH SHOW
#Puppets #TV

Only witty political marionettes could remain on French prime time TV for nearly 35 years. Since the early eighties, daily sarcastic shows have entertained the nation and fulfilled its need for public criticism: these puppets are one of the greatest illustrations of the French modern cultural landscape!

1. It all started with *Le Bébête Show*

Its characters, inspired by the British-American *Muppet Show*, took on the traits of caricatured French political figures. Introduced by journalist Stephane Collaro, it was first broadcasted in 1982 and became famous when the first national channel TF1 introduced a daily format during the 1988 presidential election: five minutes of cynicism at 7:50pm quickly attracted 30% of the audience!

Some key figures are well remembered: the frog "Kermitterrand", for example, depicted Francois Mitterrand as a megalomaniac, contemptuous personality who called himself "God"; "Black Jack", inspired by Sam the Eagle, showed a hysterical and swearing Jacques Chirac; "Pencassine", inspired by the comic character "Becassine" (but with vampire fangs) from Brittany, the province where Jean-Marie Le Pen was from; or "Amabotte" a submissive panther that represented Edith Cresson, the first woman to become French Prime Minister. While politicians felt highly offended, the public made the program a popular success for nearly 15 years.

The show, which began during Mitterrand's presidency, was eventually cancelled and died with the start of Chirac's in 1995. It slowly became a has-been after the competitive channel Canal+ introduced a more insolent and incisive alternative: *Les Guignols*.

2. *Les Guignols* takes over

Inspired by the former French *Bébête Show*, the Brits created their own satirical show *Spitting Image* in the mid-eighties, where latex puppets assassinated politicians and show business figures with a dark and severe humour. Alain de Greef, the new program director of French channel Canal+, was impressed by the tone and political sense of the English. He then decided to start a French version and approached Alain Duverne, lead artist and creator of the *Bébête Show*'s marionettes. Excited by the challenge of creating innovative latex puppets, Duverne joined de Greef: they became known as the mother and father of the new show that soon enjoyed a tremendous growth in popularity. It quickly eclipsed its rival in the early 90s after being the sole media covering the Gulf War from a snide perspective. The show had three million viewers daily and was awarded the best French entertainment programme in 1993, 1995 and 1997.

The "Super-liar" (representing Jacque Chirac), capable of uttering unbelievable lies without getting caught, "Mr Sylvestre", a caricature of an ugly and cynical American who represented the greed of the military-industrial complex, and "Homo Erectus", depicting Dominique Strauss-Kahn, shown coming out of the shower in a leopard outfit, are some of the many famous puppets of the program. This parody machine currently budgets 15 million euros every year, employing 300 people and 30 puppeteers. Every morning four to five bits news are selected, a first draft of the scenario is ready at the beginning of the afternoon and is finalised by 5pm, when puppeteers and imitators start rehearsing. At 7:55 pm, the show is recorded live, hosted by a puppet facsimile of the historical TF1 French new presenter Patrick Poivre d'Arvor.

These puppets shows have actually had tremendous impact on French pop culture, introducing many catchphrases widely adopted by the population (e.g.: "à l'insu de mon plein gré"), shaping the images of some personalities or influencing voters. Many countries or public figures have considered the parodies abhorrent, but as we say in France, "everyone can express their opinion".

ABRACARAMBAR AND CARAMELISED JOKES
#Jokes #Carambar

1. As usual, it wasn't planned (really?)

We love fairy tales, so here is another success story that started by mistake. According to the brand, founders Georges and Augustin from the chocolate factory Delespaul in Lille decided to run market studies, which were quite unusual in the early fifties. One of their studies showed that children had had enough of traditional lollipops and wanted to chew candies instead. Trying to mix chocolate with caramel, a machine went mad and unexpectedly produced a long soft caramel bar: the Carambar was born. Miraculous. Abracarambar!

60 years later, the formula hasn't changed (7cm long, 10g in a yellow packaging with twisted ends) and its success has been phenomenal. The Carambar remains the favourite sweet of youngsters, with 97% notoriety, one million units sold every day (mainly in local bakeries) for just a few cents and a trans-generational brand full of stories! A key pillar of its success was carefully cultivating its image and values, where impertinence and transgression give power to children (we still remember the iconic Aboogoodooflash ads from the eighties). Unfortunately, it generated some tensions with its various recent owners: the British Cadbury and the American KraftFoods just couldn't agree. Fortunately, a French group just bought the brand recently. Abracarambar!

2. The Jokes

A particularity of Carambar is to have a joke written inside each wrap. It became so popular for nearly 50 years that these jokes are now associated with the brand and have even passed into common speech: a "blague Carambar" actually refers to a bad childish joke! Here are a few examples:

"Where do super heroes do their shopping? In a super market."
"What do kangaroos read? They read pocket books."
"Mr and Mrs Tucky have a son, what's his name? Ken."

Since the early 2000s, anybody could submit their ideas and it proved very stimulating as thousands are received every year and 500 published on average!

In 2013, a massive media buzz took place in France and all the journalists talked about the news: following decades of criticism for the low quality of its jokes, Carambar decided to replace them by educational riddles and a countdown to the change could be seen on its website. A real shock-wave took French society by surprise. Petitions emerged to prevent the change, political figures talked about it, TV stars debated and social media went crazy. Gladly, this was the biggest joke (and a true, masterful buzz) organised by the company #itwasajoke. In a few weeks, we all understood how much we loved Carambar and how this little caramel bar with its silly humour was such a strong part of French pop culture.

Still, an existential question remained unanswered: who is writing these millions jokes? If you know an inventor of Carambar's gags, please put us in touch, we would love to talk to this unicorn and crack the mystery.

THE ROCAMBOLESQUE LIFE OF ROLAND GARROS
#Aviation #Tennis

Everybody know the French clay tennis open, one of the four tennis grand slam tournaments, but who knows the origin of the inspiring man behind its name?

1. A young bourgeois

In the nineteenth century, Garros, a member of the reigning family of French island of Réunion, moved to Saigon, Cochinchina (a historical province of South Vietnam, a French territory at the time) to open a commercial law firm, but had to send his twelve-year-old boy Roland back to France to pursue his education.

In 1900, the young descendant would then go on to live an autonomous life, and went from the famous boarding school Stanislas in Cannes to the elitist Parisian business school HEC and beyond. This early independence led him to explore all sorts of activities.

2. A passionate cloud kisser

Cycling champion at 16, he quickly developed a strong affinity for mechanical sports, joined the French automotive manufacturer Grégoire after HEC business school and quickly launched his own business: a sports car retailer (near the Arc de Triomphe!) that quickly made him wealthy. Shortly after, he had a revelation: he now wanted to be an aviator! Roland attended a fly-in near Reims, and invested the proceeds of his start-up in a flying machine.

He soon learned to pilot by himself with his Demoiselle airplane, got his license and was asked to join the New York aviation meeting in 1910 at only 22. Looking to perfect his flying skills, he toured the US, Mexico and Cuba and won his nickname: the cloud kisser!

The explorer consequently set numerous records: he was the first to fly over the tropical Amazon with Eduardo Chavos (the founding father of the Brazilian aviation), the first to climb to an altitude of 4000m and the first to cross the Mediterranean Sea between Africa and Europe. Becoming a celebrity, befriending the likes of philosopher Jean Cocteau and car manufacturer Bugatti (who built seven "Garros" models), flirting with pianist Misia Sert and Hollywood dancer Isadora Duncan, his life may have been close to Magic in the Moonlight. But WWI was around the corner...

3. A patriotic warrior

Having joined a flying squadron, he patented a special machine gun that fired through the propeller and his outstanding engineering skills helped him to specify the first single-set fighter used in the following years by all countries. He consequently went to the war front and won endless victories before being shot in 1915, crashing in Belgium and being made prisoner of war. After several attempts, Roland Garros managed to escape with a fake German uniform and the help of his Germanophile friend Marchal on an epic road trip back. His story eventually inspired the movie masterpiece *La Grande Illusion* by Jean Renoir. He received the French Légion d'Honneur by President Clemenceau and an offer to join the French Central Command, which he declined. Instead, he went back to fight again and died in 1918 at age 30.

One might wonder: what is the link with tennis? There is none! A close friend of Roland's who became president of the prestigious tennis stadium simply adopted the name, honouring forever a glorious French aviator.

RED CARPET ON LA CROISETTE
#Cannes #festival

The most famous 24 steps in the world are waiting every spring for the most brilliant film directors, recognised geniuses, acclaimed actors and emerging talents: welcome to the Cannes Festival!

1. Political and cultural ambitions

Outraged by the interference of fascist governments into the Venice Mostra selection, an international and politically independent film festival was proposed by the French Ministry of Arts. Supported by the British and Americans, the first festival was held in 1947 in Cannes, whose sunny Mediterranean coast and lavish palaces were quite attractive. In the fifties, its popularity soared due to the presence of celebrities such as Sophia Loren, Grace Kelly, Brigitte Bardot, Romy Schneider, Alain Delon, Gina Lollobrigida and many more.

Organisers selected cinematographic creations from all over the world to celebrate the diversity of the "Seventh Art". Since 1955, twenty films (aka "the Official Selection") compete every year for the prestigious Palme d'Or, awarded to the best film. The palm leaf design was actually inspired by the coat of arms of the old city and quickly became the festival's symbol, a 24-carat trophy provided by luxury jewelry house Chopard. The Grand Prix is the second-most prestigious prize of the festival while the Prix du Jury usually rewards originality or novelty. The award Un Certain Regard was created in 1978 to reward one of other selections of twenty films by promising new film directors. Finally the last award, Cinéfondation, was created in 1995 to support the entry of new writers.

2. But how is a film actually selected?

Candidate films must be finalised less than a year before the Festival, must not have participated in any other international competition and must not have been shown anywhere outside their home country.

Two committees (one for French movies, one for foreign movies) look at more than 4000 films but only twenty are short-listed (with no more than three French): the list is unveiled one month before the start.

The interesting bit is that the French committee is protected by secrecy (its members are not known) and the international committee is composed of only four members (the son of the previous general delegate, a journalist, a director and one other guy). Who is supervising and nominating the committee? A man in full power: the Delegate General.

3. The Delegate General and the Jury

Everybody knows the stars, but who knows the Delegate General? Over the last 40 years, only two men have held the position. In the seventies, Gilles Jacob got the job, promoting talented filmmakers and actors against producers and politics. Since 2004, Thierry Frémaux has been the new visionary head, the man in the shadow who not only appoints the two committees, but the president and members of the Jury too!

Composed of eight personalities and a president, the Jury is announced a week before the opening. Its mission is to choose the future winners: quite a responsibility!
Members can't disclose their positions, their discussions are kept confidential, their debates must never be revealed and extreme discretion is paramount: they don't read the newspaper, they don't watch TV, they maintain limited interactions with the outside world and anonymously attend the showings. A secret ballot is organised for their final decision, which usually happens in the luxurious Villa Domergue as it has since the eighties. In 2017, the 70th Festival was placed under the presidency of Spanish film maker, scriptwriter and producer Pedro Almodovar. The winner of the Palme d'Or was *The Square*, a Swedish satirical drama movie directed by Ruben Ostlund.

Fancy a trip to Cannes to see the two daily movie showings? Good luck!

FOOTBALLERS OR FRENCH GANGSTERS ?
#Football

Head-butts, prostitution, insults, strikes, blackmails: read the true and entertaining story of the depraved and dangerous (but talented) national squad of the new millennium (beware: for 18+ readers only).

Act.1: "Forceful" Zizou

He is violent but he is loved. Or he is loved but he is violent. Don't get me wrong, I love him too! His name is Zinedine Zidane, the former charismatic leader of the French team, world champion in 1998, Euro champion in 2000, winner of the 2002 Champions league with the Real Madrid, triple Fifa player, champion of Italy and Spain, the biggest financial transfer at the time and designated as one of the greatest players who ever existed, also known as "the Artist".

Others could call him the "Headbutter", a habit he probably got in Castellane, an area of Marseille where he and his family grew up, a neighbourhood notorious for its history of high crime. It was actually in Cannes where Zidane's first coaches noticed that he was prone to attack spectators who insulted his race. His most famous exploit may well have been during the 2006 world cup final, ending his career on a red flag after headbutting Marco Materazzi in the chest "If you look at all the red cards I had in my career, most of them were a result of provocation. This isn't justification, this isn't an excuse, but my passion, temper and blood made me react and I'd rather die than apologise".

The team consequently lost, but guess what? French still supported him and thought that wasn't a big deal. After all, we all agreed with Pele, who said "Zidane is the master. Over the past ten years, there's been no one like him, he has been the best player in the world" and even President Chirac paid him a tribute afterward.

So, was it a freak phenomenon or are French footballers borderline?

Act. 2: The Knysna Fiasco

A few years later, the trend was set. It started innocently with a young prostitute, Zahia, who was fancied by the new star of team: a lovely gentleman from the ghetto called Ribery. Oh I forgot to say, he was married with children and couldn't imagine the girl was only 16, maybe because he wasn't the one buying (his buddy Govou did, and he liked to share, as true friends do). Well, she was actually hot.

Our hero (sometimes called "Scarface") unfortunately led what was a disastrous world premiere that couldn't be done by anybody else: a strike from the national team, refusing to leave the bus to train during the 2010 World Cup in South Africa! What could Domenech (who was actually a terrible coach) have done to provoke this shocking public protest? He just sent the striker Nicolas Anelka, who had insulted him the day before ("go fuck yourself in the ass, you son of a bitch") back home.

But as the captain of team, Evra, rightly said during the following press conference "The problem of the French team isn't Anelka, it is the traitor who leaked this to the press. Only players knew and we now need to eliminate the traitor". Absolutely! [song playing: the national anthem "Allons enfants de la patrie..."]

Adidas consequently physically destroyed the "shame bus" during a TV show #Allin or #Nothing

Act 3: A little sex blackmail "to help"

After a few outraged politicians stepped in, and after what seemed to be a good clean-up with a new coach and new players, the public believed it could like the team again. A moral awakening had happened.

Hold-on. A few years later in 2015, it was unveiled that our beloved attacker Benzema was behind a little blackmail to make public intimate pictures of his colleague Valbuena: a serious crime but just a little hiccup for the President of the French football, Le Graet, who tried to minimize the affair "they are just two kids, they should have a drink, shake hands and play together again". Or maybe these young millionaire's athletes need a bit more education?

What can I say? Keep following the French team (I predict a sensational scandal in the next two years) and keep reading the newspaper *L'Equipe* (they know the insiders).

MACARONS: (DESSERT) KINGMAKERS!

#Macaron

Macarons are a must: the luxurious French sweet par excellence, that made the fame and fortune of the most brilliant chefs for a reason, they won French Kings' recognition!

1. A holy royal treat

A macaron is a French small sweet meringue-based confection made of almonds, characterized by a round shape and a wide variety of flavours. It is however extremely difficult to make: only pastry masters can bring it to life.

Also known as "the monk's belly button", some said it was invented in 791 in the Cormery convent, founded during the reign of famous French emperor Charlemagne. Others attribute its creation to Monsieur Adam, a pastry chef from Saint Jean-de-Luz, who designed it for the wedding of the Sun King Louis XIV in 1660.

It became a hit at the court and transformed this cake-shop into a prosperous family business. Then, it was also a specialty of Charles Dalloyau, who was consequently hired by King Louis XVI. Dalloyau joined the elite, receiving the very prestigious title of Officier de Bouche, the highest French gastronomy distinction at the time. His descendants were ennobled and started a culinary dynasty, founding the first French "House of Gastronomy" in 1802.

It reached another dimension in 1880 with Ladurée, one of the first tea houses of Paris, mixing the traditional Parisian café with a pastry delight and a women-friendly environment. The place soon became renowned for its flagship product: a pastel-coloured macaron.

2. Ladurée: the Vuitton of macarons

A single modest shop on rue Royale for more than 100 years, the business was bought in 1993 by the French family Holder (the Holder group also owns the bakery Paul): this was the beginning of an international success with a clever re-positioning into luxury.

In a few years, Ladurée the macaron maker was run like a "haute-couture" fashion house: two "collections" are produced every year (spring-summer and autumn-winter), the packaging is designed by John Galliano or Christian Lacroix, handmade products with the best ingredients, its shops are situated in prime locations (from Madison Avenue to Saint-Tropez or Harrods), its staff are dressed with signature outfits from Chantal Thomas and it has an army of stars for promotion: from Kate Moss to Katie Holmes, Ladurée's bags and sweets have been seen everywhere by millions!

No wonder the brand has now over 85 shops worldwide, and growing. And no wonder they hired Pierre Hermé for their new start!

3. Pierre Hermé: the "Picasso of Pastry"

The youngest person to ever be named France's Pastry Chef of the year, Pierre Hermé has been awarded the Chevalier de la Légion d'Honneur. He is without a doubt one of the first world stars of the food industry. After being pastry chef at Fauchon from 1986 to 1996, he joined Ladurée to build their success story.

And boom! Macarons unveiled his ultimate talent and he consequently gained international recognition: "Kitchen Emperor", "Pastry Provocateur" or "Magician of Tastes", to name a few titles. A few years later, he was ready to build his own story: the Maison Pierre Hermé was born in 1997. Here is how he describes one of his signature dishes:

"Macarons only weigh a few grams, but that's enough to leave your senses quivering with pleasure. Their thin, crisp shell, slightly rounded shape, tempting colours and tender interiors draw devotees to devour them with their eyes, and caress their smooth surface. Their flavours solicit the nose and, when one bites into that crisp shell, the ears tingle with pleasure and the palate is finally rewarded."

Well, you're now probably ready to have a bite, but no worries if no travel to Paris is lined-up: we found a true London little gem in Islington! Give the macarons of Belle Époque a try: if you don't melt for them, we'll give you your money back.

THE FESTIVAL OF AVIGNON: 70 YEARS OF THEATER AND CREATION

#Theatre

1. The world's largest performing arts event

The Festival of Avignon can almost be summed up as seven decades dedicated to preserving cultural heritage and encouraging contemporary creation! It has become one of the oldest and most important performing arts events in the world, with over tens of thousands enjoying outdoor performances in Provençal summer nights.

It is above all a festival of creation, as new acts represent more than two thirds of the programming, and there is at least one show premiere every evening throughout three entire weeks in July. Featuring the best playwrights and actors working in contemporary productions, more than 50 different shows are performed each year, of which half are plays, but dance, musical, poetry or multidisciplinary are also honoured. Most pieces actually originate from countries and authors outside of France, offering a gateway into artists' own world and an immersion into various languages and cultures.

The Festival is more than a popular event. Despite being partly financed by the French Ministry of Fine Arts, by the EU commission and other various artistic bodies, it maintains complete independence, successfully bringing together the general public and international creation. By fully financing all the performances for a month, everyone can have access to the world living culture!

2. Avignon : the ultimate city-theatre

What's also amazing about the festival is Avignon's breath-taking scenery: it is an ancient city where seven successive popes lived in the 1300s, a stunning UNESCO World Heritage site, all entirely dedicated to the performing arts with open-air stages facing historical venues.

From the small cloister of the Celestine religious order, a singular place with its two magnificent plane trees planted in its centre, to the spectacular Honorary Court of the Popes' Palace where the Festival's first play was directed, to the former quarry of Boulbon, Avignon's remarkable and fascinating locations inspire directors, artists and spectators.

Each summer, Avignon offers its heritage and truly becomes the ultimate city-theatre, to our greatest pleasure!

3. A glorious rise in a few distinct steps

It all started in 1947 with one man: Jean Vilar. An actor and director, he devoted himself to creating a type of theatre different from the elitist scene that could be seen in Paris at the time, in order to "renew theatre and collective forms of art by providing a more open space (...) to give a breath of fresh air; to reconcile architecture with dramatic poetry". For 17 years his aim was to attract a young and captive audience with stage pioneers.

From 1964 onward, Vilar opened the Festival to other disciplines (dance with Maurice Béjart, musical theatre with Orden). Public interest kept growing as well as the desire of various companies to get exposure: that was the beginning of the Off festival, where local or young troupes not selected by the Festival committee also wanted to present their work. Nowadays the Off welcomes over 3000 companies who put on shows in about a hundred different spots!

In 1980, the Festival reached a turning point under the lead of young administrator Bernard Faivre d'Arcier: the Festival transformed into one of the biggest enterprises in the performing arts. Modern and professional, it was ready to expand, attracting world-renowned talents and becoming an international hub of contemporary culture.

Today the Festival opened its doors to works of traditional and contemporary culture from outside of Europe, but also remained at the centre of French stage creation with well-known directors like Jacques Lassalle and a new generation represented by Olivier Py, as well as choreographers such as Angelin Prejlocaj.

Touring the South East of France this summer? If you stop by Avignon, you will enjoy the new theme of this year.

TOUR DE FRANCE: A MEDIA MACHINE
#Cycling

The second most watched sports event on the planet, the three-week Tour de France attracts an average TV viewership of 2.6 billion every July! Here is the story of cycling's most-famous Grand Tour.

1. A newspaper's "coup"

In 1903, the magazine *L'Auto* faced sluggish circulation and a young journalist and cycling writer, Geo Lefevre, suggested a race around France, bigger than anything done before, to increase exposure and paper sales! The French annual multiple-stage bicycle race was born, initially with a 6-day competition.

It proved a massive success and the magazine's circulation doubled to 65,000 after the first Tour, and increased to a nearly a million copies a few years later. It appealed to the public from the start not just for the challenge but because it stimulated the French to know more about their country (academic historians say most people in France had little idea of the shape of their country until *L'Auto* began publishing maps of the race). The race leader's yellow jersey ("maillot jaune") was actually instituted during the first editions of the race to reflect the distinctive yellow paper used for printing the magazine!

L'Auto stopped publishing during World War II, but its successor started soon after: *L'Equipe*, which is nowadays the French leading sport newspaper. Media tycoon Amaury bought the paper in 1968, and founded ASO (Amaury Sport Organisation) bringing the Tour de France to another level and taking over other international sports events such as La Vuelta in Spain or the Dakar Rally.

2. The race

Of the three three-week Grand Tour races (including the Giro of Italy and the Vuelta of Spain), the Tour de France is the oldest and most prestigious.

While the route changes each year, the 21 day-long race stays the same with time trials, the passage through the mountain chains of the Pyrenees and the Alps, and the finish on the Champs-Élysées: 3500 kilometres covered by 20 teams of 9 riders competing for the best general time (yellow jersey), the best sprinters and the best climbers. Winning a stage is also one of the most prominent successes a rider can earn in his career.

But being last isn't bad either: the rider who has taken most time is called the "red lantern" (after the red light at the back of a vehicle) and can ask high fees to participate to the races that follow the Tour! But no worries, those who can't continue the race are collected by the "brush-car" before going back home.

To host a stage start or finish brings prestige to a town and a few spots also belong to the myth of Tour: as such the climb of L'Alpe d'Huez, of the Tourmalet or of the Galibier!

3. The caravan

With millions of fans lining the route, the course brings a festival mood along the road, fuelled by the caravan that precedes the riders. At its height between 1930 and the mid-1960s, before television was established, advertisers competed to attract public attention (for instance, accordionist Yvette Horner performed on the roof of a Citroën during entire stages and became the lead entertainer during the daily evening ball for 11 years, a record!).

The popular spirit was progressively transformed in the seventies by the sponsors, and as the writer Pierre Bost wrote: "This caravan of 60 gaudy trucks singing across the countryside the virtues of an apéritif, a maker of underpants or a dustbin is a shameful spectacle. It bellows, it plays ugly music, it's sad, it's ugly, it smells of vulgarity and money."

But hey, with an average of 250 promotional vehicles each year spending between 200,000–€500,000 each, a commercial cash machine was born and this isn't even counting the TV ads: here we are, the French did invent the sport business with Le Tour!

Still, the magic goes on and we can't help watching some of the most beautiful landscapes on earth. People are always drawn to the epic, and the Tour provides it.

THE LEGION OF HONOUR: A PRESTIGIOUS FRENCH SYMBOL
#Prestige

"The Legion of Honour is rewarding eminent merits for the nation". The story behind this ultimate French national reward is captivating: while mainly symbolic (devotion, courage and sacrifice have no price, after all), this centenary decoration is a strong element of French heritage.

1. A history of "Honour and Fatherland"

Knights' orders and decorations servicing an ideal have had a long history in France. Inspired by the Middle Age religious movements or by the popular order of Saint-Louis (created by King Louis XIV to reward military Catholic officers), Napoleon Bonaparte, First Consul of France, decided to create a new order after the Revolution.

In 1802, the "Legion of Honour" quickly resumed as a new symbol of the Empire, grew in popularity by including civilians and women (not exclusive to the military anymore) and became the sole French national order in 1830.

In the sixties, General de Gaulle modernized the national honours, adding a second order "of Merit" to reward more distinguished people and strengthen the prestige of the first one.

Now deeply anchored within the French identity, the Legion of Honour is awarded to famous personalities and unknown citizens alike: the heroes of the Nation, aren't they?

2. How to get your medal in a few steps

Only 3000 people a year receive a Legion of Honour, 2000 of which are civilians, so what's the path? To start with, you need to know what is an "eminent merit". Well, it's a bit blurred as it can range from "the depth of your human journey to an act of generosity or an action favouring national interest". However the candidate should also be recognizable as a role model and must have 20 years of service to the cause (no wonder the average age of recipients is 58!).

If you believe you bring benefits through your economic, scientific, educational, artistic, diplomatic or sportive activities and don't want to wait that long, a couple of shortcuts exist:

- **Method 1** (your best bet) submit a "citizen initiative". Since 2007, anyone can apply if they gather 50 signatures. This is a much better alternative than waiting for the authorities to notice you, and as only 15% of the applications are dismissed, you've just increased your odds!

- **Method 2** (a bit more challenging) benefit from the few "exceptional propositions" (saving someone from death or winning a Gold medal at the Olympics qualify).

- **Method 3** (unlikely) be a foreign head of state and tie the award to big contracts to pass the "moral value" test (Vladimir Putin got his in 2006, Nasser al Thani the Qatar Prime Minister in 2009, and Prince Muhamad Bin Nayef of Saudi Arabia in 2016). But at that stage, do you really care?

It is worth mentioning that you can decline, like French economist Thomas Piketty did in 2015 "I refuse this nomination because I don't think this is the role of a government to decide who is honourable. The state should better spend its time to boost growth in France and Europe instead of distributing those distinctions".

3. Behind the scenes

There are two key leading figures. The Grand Master is the French President: he has an ultimate say on each topic, nominates the board members of the orders and appoints the Grand Chancellor.

In fact, the latter is the real person in charge: guardian of the code, arbitrator of the decisions, president of the boards, museum director, and rector of the national elite girls boarding schools (aka the "Maisons d'Education"), he chairs the institution for six years and ranks 17th in the French protocol order. Only military generals are appointed, and since 2016 General Benoit Puga has been the 33rd Grand Chancellor.

Want to know more? Put the glamorous Palace of Salm at the agenda of your next Paris trip: this is the headquarters of the order and the largest museum in the world dedicated to chivalry orders. A glorious place for sure.

ORANGINA PULP FICTION
#Drink

How do you shake-up the bottle, and the market? Throw audacious TV ads that consistently alternate from sexiness to humour, you'll connect with your audience and conquer the world! It actually worked for the most famous French soft drink: Orangina.

1. "One day, our orange juice will be known all over the globe"

The visionary Léon Béton said this in the thirties referring to his juiceries of French Algeria. He had just come back from a business trip in Marseille where he had bought a recipe from Spanish doctor Trigo Mirallès. The 'Naranjina', a mixture of orange and sparkling water, was soon renamed 'Orangina'. Sold in a funky, bulbous bottle in the shape of an orange, it became an instant hit in the colony, relocating its operation to the Riviera in the early sixties to take over the national market.

With very strict requirements of sugar, acidity, colour, texture and a blend of five different types of oranges from Africa and Europe, its recipe was a well-kept secret. Still, the challenge faced by the Béton family was three fold: bottling an unusual shape, facing fierce competition from Coca Cola (which was just entering the French market) and, most challenging, convincing bar owners. The latter were not keen: glasses were full of pulp and not easy to wash, bottles were not standard and not easy to store.

The Béton family said "the only thing we have to do is to convince consumers", and so they did: with audacious advertising campaigns.

2. Advertising with humour and eroticism

Orangina started its communication with two key identity factors: the bottle and the orange peel. Popular designs of the poster maker Bernard Villemot (who created over 17 visuals during 30 years) anchored the brand in people's minds with refreshing symbols: sea, sun and fun.

But the true genius came with the TV ads. Novel at the time, Béton empowered young talented movie directors to create brand clips focusing on "shaking the bottle": this was a smash hit. The first video, "a barman habit" by Jean-Jacques Annaud won the Golden Lion at the Venice advertising festival in 74.

Following its acquisition by Pernod-Ricard, Orangina started its international expansion with the support of sexy sensual campaigns targeting a younger audience. The first was in 1984 with "The Swimming Pool", then in 1989, Orangina became the first company to sponsor musical songs and Latin dances such as 'Lambada' (3.5 million discs sold): these were massive successes too.

In the need to expand further, the company used black humour to seduce teens: this was the beginning of the crazy bottle-men stories from French author Alain Chabat. It would go on for a decade!

In 2008, a new series of commercials featuring anthropomorphic animals re-entered the sexual realm and caused outrage for its suggestive content (such as spraying the drink onto the breasts of other animals, or riding bottles which then exploded). Censored in the UK, the advert proved popular with millions of views online, creating yet another buzz.

Following the pattern, the humour came back with the catchphrase "shake the world".

So yes, with several billion units sold per year worldwide, we concur with the British: "Orangina, c'est shook."

MR BRAINWASH: THE NEW ANDY WARHOL
#PopArt

In the matter of a few weeks, a French street pop artist took Los Angeles by storm. Described by Banksy as "a phenomenon", he sold $1 million worth of artwork at his first exhibition, reached instant fame and consequently designed album covers for Madonna and Michael Jackson to name a few! What's the story behind him?

1. The birth of a (controversial) icon

Thierry Guetta was born in the south of France. He moved to the US later to open a clothing shop, to enjoy life with his family and to put everything on tape: Thierry was a bit obsessive with videos; he recorded pretty much everything.

Thanks to his cousin, the famous street artist nicknamed Invader, he discovered the underground world of street art. Offering his services to produce the first ever documentary of this mysterious scene, he got to know all the rising stars, filming them during days and nights for many years.

After the documentary was finally done, he was inspired: why not become an artist himself?

2. *Exit through the gift shop*

Nobody thought he would find a new passion, or obsession. He now called himself Mr Brainwash (aka MBW), and what happened next made history.

MBW kindly asked two legends to endorse him. They were friends, so they did. What they didn't know was the scale of the project: he re-mortgaged his business to rent the former CBS studio (several thousand square feet) and hired an entire production team to create pieces of art under his supervision. What they didn't expect either was to see themselves quoted on massive billboards all over LA.

"Mr. Brainwash is a force of nature, he's a phenomenon. And I don't mean that in a good way."
- Banksy

"Mr. Brainwash is an enigma. He is awesome, infuriating, almost impossible to define."
- Shepard Fairey

The move proved spectacular. All the newspapers started to talk about him and Mr Brainwash made the front cover of LA Weekly, the largest publication of the West Coast. His first exhibition *Life is Beautiful* opened in June 2008. Initially planned for two weeks, it extended to three months, attracting a total of 50,000 visitors who lined the streets for blocks. In less than six months, an artist was born, selling his art pieces for $1 million.

The story was actually covered by the fascinating Academy Award documentary *Exit though the gift shop*. And it did not take long before a crucial question arose: was it the biggest prank in art history?

3. "Maybe art is a bit of a joke?"

In 2010, Mr Brainwash's second show in NYC covered 15,000 square feet. In 2011 he sold out his London exhibition within two days. From Art Basel in 2013 to Rita Ora's live musical performances in 2015, attracting hundreds of thousands of visitors to his enormous multi-storey warehouse solo art shows or creating cover artwork for Madonna or Michael Jackson, the list goes on forever: Mr Brainwash is actually no joke! We can say he has been pushing the limits of twenty-first century pop culture and he may well be right when he said with a smile "I am Banksy's biggest work of art".

Here is what Banksy thinks: "maybe he's been a genius all along, maybe he's been a bit lucky... maybe it means art is a bit of a joke... I don't think Thierry plays by the rule, in some ways, but then there aren't supposed to be any rules. I always used to encourage anyone I met to make art; I used to think anyone should do it... I don't really do that so much anymore."

Well, the debate is obviously still valid: what is art? #brainwashing

"CLASSES PREPAS" AKA THE FRENCH CRAMMING

#School

If you are a French student willing to get the best national engineering or business schools, you'll have to become a mole ("un taupin") for two to three years: don't expect to see to see the sun, get ready to be mistreated and join the very peculiar French prep schools "classes préparatoires". After that, you'll officially earn three main attributes.

1. You'll be a nerd

After the baccalaureate, only 5% of the French students go into these "classes préparatoires" or "classes prépas" that will prepare and train them to enrol in one of the "Grandes Écoles", the French elite schools producing most of France's scientists, executives and intellectuals, in that order.

In that order, because the scientific way of life has the highest status. Mathematics and science are indeed regarded as the most difficult, and hence attracting the best of the best. This is the royal way, and no wonder more than half of French CEO's are engineers (a very French specificity).

Why not after all? Well… the workload is one of the highest in the world, averaging 10 hours contact a day plus 6 hours written exams and 2 hours of "colles" (see below) a week. Of course this doesn't account for the homework that fills all your remaining free time. When you are 18 and are willing to spend the entire next two years of your life in your room, you definitely qualify as a nerd.

Need more proof? The students are nicknamed "un demi" (one half) in the first year, "trois demis" (three halves) during their first second-year and "cinq demis" (five halves) if you redo your second year. Why? Easy, 3/2 is the value of the integral of x from 1 to 2, and 5/2 is the value of the integral of x from 2 to 3. Yes, they are big nerds. :)

2. You'll be a masochist

On top of an insane and exceptionally high workload (think 16 hours of maths, 12 hours of physics, 12 hours chemistry and a bit of other stuff every week), students have to complete an oral examination two to three times a week in groups of three. In front of a blackboard, facing a professor alone in a room, they are verbally assaulted by the sadistic examiner whose aim is to give them the hardest problems to solve. They consequently will be stuck ("collé") and insulted for being stupid (so they learn to be tough). This session is therefore called a "colle" and quite unique to this French education. We told you, only masochists go there!

3. You'll be an elitist

You'll pay the price, but you'll usually get admitted into the prestigious and selective "Grandes Écoles", the elite schools (École Polytechnique, ENS, HEC, and so on) which often have roots in the seventeenth and eighteenth century (they aimed at graduating military officers).

These top-rated schools, which the French praise for being "généraliste" (interdisciplinary), traditionally produce most of France's high-ranking civil servants, politicians and executives. There is actually a well-known phenomenon of consanguinity within the French ruling class: more than 80% of it comes from there, and outsiders find it hard to penetrate the circle. It's sometimes less about talent than belonging, no wonder they are a bit elitist.

GEORGES BRASSENS, SINGING POET

#Music

Brassens, with his rock star moustache, his pipe, his guitar and his warm southern accent, became one of the most popular French musicians of the sixties. Singing more than a hundred poems, mostly of his own composition, he was one of the only singers to receive the grand prize of poetry from the French Academy.

1. A rebel from the South

Born near Montpellier in Sete (where his museum is), Brassens wasn't the most studious pupil: he was a young fighter who preferred small larcenies to school before finally getting caught at 16. He was forgiven by his father: that was a turning point. Later, he paid him a tribute with his song *Les Quatre Bacheliers* (*The Four Students*) but with a tarnished reputation, young Georges decided to leave for Paris, despite the war having just started.

At 22 he was sent to Germany by the Vichy government to work in a plane factory near Berlin in Basdorf (being the obliged duty of young men under occupied France). But Brassens escaped in March.

During 1944, he had to hide from the Gestapo, staying at his Aunt's in a modest house. "I was well there and since that time, I keep an exceptional resistance to discomfort". He stayed there 22 years, composing many songs.

2. An engaged poet

Alphonse Bonnafe, his French teacher, is the man who inspired him into writing poetry. More at ease with words than with music, his talent was discovered by Patachou, the owner of a cabaret in Montmartre, where the artistic director of Philips was seduced and offered him a contract. The newspaper headlines declared "a poet is discovered"! In 1953 he started at Bobino, a theatre that would become his second home.

Fourteen albums were recorded between 1952 and 1976 with countless popular French songs, often decrying hypocrisy and self-righteousness in the conservative French society of the time, especially among the religious, the well-to-do, and those in law enforcement. Extremely demanding, he reworked his texts over and over, changing a word, an image, until he felt the tone was perfect.

Brassens triumphed. His most famous songs included *Les Copains d'Abord* (*Friendship First*), *La Mauvaise Reputation* (*Bad Reputation*), *Les Amoureux des Bancs Publics* (*Young Lovers on Public Benches*) and so many more.

3. Death

After years of sickness and painful renal colic, Brassens passed away in late October, 1981 at age sixty, generating an immense shock wave throughout the country, well summarized by TV news presenter Patrick Poivre d'Arvor: "we are all here, a bit stupid, at 20, at 40, at 60...we lost an uncle". At least, he witnessed the victory of one of his social fights, for which he wrote the popular song *Le Gorille* (*The Gorilla*): the death penalty was abolished three weeks earlier.

THE FRENCH "HAUTE-COUTURE"
#Fashion

Paris invented the high-end fashion houses, the avant-garde dressmakers who showed the world what luxury and glamor mean. But very few know that an English man, Charles Worth, was the true father of Haute-Couture, revolutionising the French fashion industry at its start.

1. The legacy of French style

Nobody can argue: France has set the standard of style and fashion for centuries. It all started with Louis XIV in Versailles, where talented fashion designers established their reputation. The place blossomed as the world fashion reference.

In 1770, fashion trader Rose Bertin established "Le Grand Mogol", in the rue du Faubourg Saint-Honoré in Paris, and quickly became the trend setter at the King's court, gaining the title of "Minister of Fashion" and boosting the Parisian industry.

He was followed by the official supplier of Napoleon, Louis Leroy, who led a renowned House on rue Richelieu. In the mid-nineteenth century, Paris was the established fashion capital with over 2400 tailors, but an Englishman was ready to take it to another level.

2. The birth of Haute-Couture

Although born in Lincolnshire, Charles Worth made his mark in the French fashion industry. He revolutionised dressmaking by making the dressmaker an artist of garnishment and of one-of-a-kind designs. He is best known for preparing a portfolio of designs that were shown on live models at the House of Worth, near Place Vendome, creating the Fashion shows and introducing the concept of fashion collections.

In 1869, Worth also created a Fashion Collective that aimed at protecting its members from illegal copy makers. This organisation became the official syndicate of the industry in 1911, formally establishing the art of Haute-Couture.

3. La Mode Française

Since that time, "Haute-Couture" has meant the creation of exclusive custom-fitted clothing, made by hand from start to finish and from the highest quality and most expensive fabrics.

In the early twentieth century, many designers followed Worth, joining the first wave of French Haute-Couture: Chanel, Lanvin, Dior and Balenciaga, to name of few. In the 1960s, a group of young designers left these establishments and opened their own Houses, starting the Golden wave: Yves Saint Laurent, Pierre Cardin and Emanuel Ungaro were some of them. They were followed by a third wave in the eighties: Christian Lacroix, Jean-Paul Gaultier or Thierry Mugler.

Rare are the designers who can claim the "Haute-Couture" title. For the 2017 season, there were only 15 official members, endorsed by existing fellow members of the Syndicate, and committed to design two hand-made collections. Welcome to the glamorous Paris Fashion Weeks for the Spring/Summer collection in January and Autumn/Winter in July, when hundreds of shows and catwalks, in sumptuous (but highly secretive) places, set the trends of tomorrow!

So much glamour is not profitable, but preserves traditional artisans (such as the embroider Lesage or plumassier Lemarié) and French heritage. No worries, it's also an efficient brand image strategy to promote the House's main source of income: their ready-to-wear clothes (that have their own Fashion Weeks by the way).

WHY CONCORDE IS MORE FRENCH THAN BRITISH
#Aviation

The iconic plane, the Concorde, was negotiated as an international treaty between the two countries, and both the French and the Brits took great pride in it. Unfortunately for the Brits, the French did in fact abuse them a little bit, here is why.

First round: how the French made the Brits work for them

Beautifully designed with its droop nose, the plane was one of the only and best supersonic transporters ever built, flying at twice the speed of sound (Mach 2) and operated for nearly thirty years until early 2000.

It took a while to solve the many engineering challenges involved. In the UK, the Royal Aircraft Establishment (RAE) started working on it in the early fifties with the firm "Bristol", and completed a first design 10 years later. By that time, France had appointed its own company "Sud" to do the same. Because of the high costs, the two met to compare their outputs. Bristol was surprised and impressed to find that Sud had designed a very similar aircraft and came to the same conclusions in terms of economics: they were ready to collaborate and push for a joint project. The plane would be truly European! At the time, the UK was in fact pressing to enter the European Common Market, controlled by Charles de Gaulle, who kept blocking them. To get the political favours of France, the Brits politicians proposed to build a joint innovative plane and secretly leaked ten years of advanced technical research (stamped "for UK eyes only") to the French: they gave the French public credibility and got the support from their own teams – cheeky!

In 1962, an international treaty was signed rather than a commercial agreement, with heavy penalties for pulling out. In other words, the Brits worked hard for the French: 1–0 (and the French could start building it in Toulouse).

Second round: how the Brits accepted a French name

Concord, a word that means agreement, harmony or union was proposed by Harold Macmillan. But de Gaulle rejected it, and the French version was accepted (!) by the English: Minister for Technology Tony Bern announced that it would be changed to Concorde (the French version). Facing a nationalist uproar, Benn tried to explain that the suffixed "e" represented Excellence, England, Europe and Entente (Cordiale).
Well, if you wish, but: 2–0.

Third round: yet to come, BAE vs Airbus

The plane was a symbol, but it was also a financial disaster. Only Air France and British Airways operated it, and a decision was finally taken to stop it after the terrible July 2000 crash and 9/11.

The story is not over though. Airbus just trademarked "Concorde 2" (3–0 ?) and announced its intention to build a top speed 4.5 Mach plane, that will fly from Paris to NYC in 1 hour. BAE consequently invested in a company called Reaction Engines (building a Mach 5 jet to link London and Sydney in 4h only). We look forward to seeing who will get off the ground first.

The UK/French love affair is definitely not going to end anytime soon.

THE MACRONS: A COUGAR AND MOZART?

#President

Much has been written about the new French presidential couple, but here is a new insightful perspective on the story: a must-read story to know to truth behind their controversial relationship! (Spoiler: there is a bit of gossip involved)

1. Who is Brigitte?

A 40-year-old mother falling in love and having desire for her 15 year old pupil can hardly deny being a Cougar, can she?

Some will argue that the term implies pure sexual attraction, dismissing the undeniable emotional aspect that a 20+ year's relationship has confirmed. Other will explain that 25 years gap is not a big deal and that nobody questions the same age difference between Donald Trump and his wife. Some will explain that in France, the age of sexual majority is 15 anyway. Other will see the depraved morals of the French (even worse when they are Presidents).

Well, indeed, but... a) when there is a relation of authority (e.g.: teachers) an offense can be proclaimed by law; b) he wasn't an adult, and age difference does actually matter when a child or teen is involved: would you accept a 40 year old male teacher to date your 15-year-old daughter? You would probably see this man as a potential paedophile abusing his position of power, because at 15, teens are just easy to manipulate, they haven't yet experienced the realm of relationships which often makes them a bit naive and innocent; c) how can a grown-up develop romantic feelings for the classmate of her own kid? A fantastic topic for a psychoanalyst; d) France is not the "country of love" for nothing!

Let's explore further what happened.

2. Who is Emmanuel?

The key questions before judging should be: what did really happen, who seduced whom and how? According to what has been reported in the press, Emmanuel just impressed the woman, who said: "I found myself in awe of his exceptional intelligence, a way of thinking that I had never ever seen before. You know, the day when we wrote that play together, I had the feeling I was working with Mozart!"

Hard to believe, isn't it? Hello! The guy is the new French president at 39! Only Napoleon was older when he took over the country: do you think for a second he was a normal 15-year-old nerd? The man has been described as exceptionally bright by everyone.

During his short life, he has already become a philosopher, a private banker who made millions, a writer who can recite classic poetry on the go, the French Minister of Economy, and a man who smashed the political world with a new party in less than a year before being elected President!

In other words, we bet he was the one manipulating Brigitte when he was 15, and not the other way around, duh!

3. The Singularity

The issue concerns the "romantic" description of the story done by the media, who forget to remind everyone of the unusual character behind: Emmanuel (whose name literally means "God with us") is definitely an exception, a singularity per se. This type of encounter doesn't usually end up like that in real life (sorry to be a party pooper). Dismissing the fact that they are in fact the exception to the rule sends a very dangerous message to a fragile young population, who could be tempted to find that type of "romance" in general acceptable, exposing themselves to the many real sexual predators around.

Anyway, let's blame the media, hats off to the couple, and to the French: let's be En Marche for the next elections to come!

THE FRENCH FIFTH REPUBLIC
#Institutions

After a busy 2017 election period (a new President and MPs), isn't it a good time to remember what the Fifth Republic is about? Here is a snapshot of its history, its Presidential monarchy and its low parliamentary chamber (aka the "National Assembly").

1. Birth of the Fifth Republic

The Fourth Republic was established after WWII and the Parliament got all the power at the time, but this arrangement wasn't appreciated by one powerful man, General Charles de Gaulle.

In May 1958, after four years of civil war in Algeria (then a colony), French General Massu led a military coup to take over the local French government, accused of being complaisant with the rebels fighting for independence. His parachutists even took control of Corsica. Paris was afraid: what if the capital was at risk?

The former Chief of the Resistance, Charles de Gaulle (CDG), was called for help and appointed head of the Counsel (then the Parliament). But there was one condition: changing the Constitution, hence creating a new Republic that was finally born in October 1958 after being approved by referendum. CDG was now ready to be elected President in "a democratic putsch"!

2. Presidential Powers

Under the influence of CDG, the new Constitution reduced the power of the Parliament and gave executive power to the President. Here were the main changes:

The Parliament is now under control, cannot decide its agenda and can only block the Government with an absolute majority.

The President:
- is now elected directly by the citizens
- appoints the Prime Minister and its Ministers (the Government) who propose the laws
- can dissolve the main chamber of the Parliament
- can call for referendums
- is head of the army

- nominates Generals, Ambassadors, Préfets (state representatives in each region of the country) and CEOs of public companies
- cannot be tried or condemned during his mandate
- can take "full powers" in the case of a "serious crisis"
- leads the foreign policy

The Prime Minister (nominated by the President) can force the adoption of a law (Art. 49.3).

No wonder the system is sometimes called a "Republican Monarchy".

3. The Parliament

Is split in two: the lower chamber (National Assembly) of 577 MPs directly elected by the citizens, and the higher chamber (Senate) of 321 members indirectly elected.

The French Parliament votes and amends the laws. The Assemblée Nationale, its bigger chamber, is located at the Palais Bourbon, a palace worth visiting in central Paris. MPs hold office from October to June, every Tuesday, Wednesday and Thursday. MPs are elected for 5 years (like the President), one month after him. In a nutshell, if the party of the President doesn't get the majority in the Parliamentary elections, there is trouble ahead as every new law will be properly challenged or blocked.

So, let's watch: #EnMarche got the absolute majority in the 2017 Parliamentary elections with more than 289 MPs: Macron may become the next Napoleon. How exciting!

Sources: online researches, various media

Printed in Poland
by Amazon Fulfillment
Poland Sp. z o.o., Wrocław